Whose Shoes Are YOU WEARING?

Dear Jessica,
We appreciate
your support of
the "Whose Shoes"
Movement. Keep
walking in your
shoes"
Julian

Whose Shoes Are
YOU WEARING?

12 STEPS to Uncovering the
Woman You *Really* Want to Be

CHRISTINE K. ST. VIL & JULIAN B. KIGANDA

Dear Jessica,
Thank you so much for
your support! Always so
fun seeing you. Always so
Hope this book inspires
you to always walk
in your own
shoes (as you
do so well ☺)
much love & blessings,
Christine

KKULA
MEDIA

KKULA MEDIA   WASHINGTON, DC   2014

PUBLISHED & DESIGNED BY KKULA MEDIA

www.whoseshoesbook.com

Cover photographs, Eye Imagery Studios; www.eye-imagery.com

ISBN 978-0-9960978-0-2 (paperback)

ACKNOWLEDGEMENTS

There are so many people to thank for this project. First and foremost, we give thanks to God for using us and our experiences to uplift and guide others. We are a living testament to the fact that through Him, all things are possible. We want to say a very special thanks to Maama and Taata Kiganda. Mom, Dad, your love, support, guidance, and gift of faith have been invaluable as we have grown into women who are now boldly walking in our own shoes. To our siblings, Mary, Lucy, Evelyne, John, and Bruno: we appreciate the love and love you right back! Thank you.

CHRISTINE: To my husband, Phillip, who is my king and my hero: thank you for encouraging me and believing in me even when I didn't believe in myself. I am forever grateful for your unwavering love for me and our children. To my babies, Phillip Jr., Olivia, and Brielle: Mommy loves you so much, and I hope I make you as proud as you make me every day.

JULIAN: Natalia, you were on my mind when I was writing this book. As your mother, I want you to have the strongest foundation possible when it's time for you to finally leave the nest and go out into the world to use the gifts that God has graced you with. Thank you for being a reminder, every day, of joy, faith, perseverance, and miracles.

To my best friend, Heather: we've seen each other through so much, and for your friendship, I am grateful. I hope this book helps you along your own journey.

For all of those whom we have not listed by name (there are so many, and you know who you are): thank you for playing a part in this road we have traveled called "life." Your love, friendship and support mean everything. We are truly blessed.

TABLE OF CONTENTS

Whose Shoes Are
YOU WEARING?

A LETTER TO YOU

Dear Daughter,

Let it go. Let go of all the expectations and be open to the unknown. Let go of all the complicated and be open to the simple. Let go of having to know and be open to all the possibilities that I have to offer you. Your life is waiting for you—it's yours for the taking.

You've begun the true journey of faith. You've taken that first step, but there are still those old habits and thoughts that hiccup your progress. Be conscious of them, recognize them, address them, and be on your way. "For I know the plans that I have for you. Plans to prosper you and not to harm you. To give you a future and a hope."

Your job is to continue transforming and be present—fully present—at every stage of your transformation. And to be open to a change of plans.

Stop looking for permission from others and instead realize that the answers already lie within. You just need to tap into them. Be fearless. That is your motto. Be fearless because you know that you never walk alone. You already have everything you need—you just need to claim it.

You are fearfully and wonderfully made. Never forget that. I, the Lord your God, will lead you to that place of peace, joy, fulfillment, and contentment. But you have to first recognize your own sacredness.

You are beautiful and worthy of love and respect, from everyone, including yourself. Learn to say "no" when your spirit does. Learn to say "yes" when you are in alignment with your purpose. Don't let fear hold you back.

For you serve no one by playing small. The life you want is already here. You just have to claim it.

Love,
Your Heavenly Father

P.S. I've got a new pair of shoes waiting for you at the end of this journey.

INTRODUCTION

Hello, I'm Christine. And I'm Julian. We're two sisters who have traveled a long, winding path—individually and together—to become the women we've always wanted to be. It's an ongoing process, but one we now appreciate so much more and want to share with you because we're passionate about helping you discover and walk powerfully in your own shoes.

If you're reading this book, then you're probably where we were not too long ago: feeling stuck in a rut and unable to figure out which way is up. The truth is, it's not going to be easy. Nothing worth having is. You're going to want to quit, curse, and kick something at some point during this journey. If you don't, check your pulse.

But you've got to put it in your head—and your heart—that quitting is *not* an option. Not this time. Not if you want to get off of the hamster's wheel and finally move on to better things. Not if you want to live the life you've always dreamt about. Not if you have a song in you that is just dying to get out. (Just know that, for some of you, that song may come in a different form than an actual vocal performance. Not all of us were blessed with Jennifer Hudson's vocal chords.)

If you're not already setting goals and creating a plan to reach those goals, then that dream is just a hallucination. But we're here to tell you that it's possible to make it a reality. How do we know this?

We've experienced it ourselves, and we're going to teach you how.

Keep in mind that this is a journey. We want to shake you up, keep it real, but most of all, make you act upon the wishes, dreams, and goals you've been sitting on while waiting for the right time, for something to click—the heavens to open, the choir to sing, the Red Sea to part. Errrr . . . it doesn't work that way, unless you're Moses. Or Jesus. And even *He* had to take initiative before he was celebrated as the *One*.

At the end of every chapter, you will find simple exercises for you to complete to move you along your path to purposefulness and the quest for the shoes God made uniquely for you. We recommend buying yourself a journal to write your thoughts in as you go through this book. Visit us at **www.whoseshoesbook.com** to download *free* worksheets for each chapter. While you're there, let us know your thoughts on the book. We'd love to hear from you and find out what has resonated with you and helped move you from procrastination to purpose.

The main caveat of this journey is that *you have to do the work.* It's time. Someone out there needs what you have. Someone is waiting on you to use your gift to help them shine. Someone's life is going to be made better because of *you*. As you embark on this journey, remember something very important:

 TWEET THIS! @WhoseShoesBook
God doesn't ask us to be PERFECT. He asks us to be WILLING. #whoseshoes

So in the famous words of Marvin Gaye, "Let's get it on!"

xoxo Christine & Julian

1 KEEPING IT REAL: REMOVING THE WEAVE, THE LASHES, AND THE HEELS

JULIAN

Everything will line up perfectly when knowing and living truth is more important than looking good. —Alan Cohen

Have you ever had one of those moments when you wanted to smack yourself upside the head because you kept making the same mistake? I mean, you have everything else together in your life, why can't you just get this one thing right? (Or maybe two or three things . . .)

As a recovering perfectionist, I know this scenario all too well. I've always struggled with the idea of making a mistake. I think growing up in a strict African household, with an emphasis on performance and outward appearances, contributed to this disease of perfectionism, but, I take accountability for the way I internalized what success meant to me. Instead of defining it for myself, I allowed other people and their expectations—in both my personal and professional life—to dictate what my priorities should be. I tried to fit my feet in other people's ill-fitting shoes.

What others thought about my hair, my clothes, my choice of friends, my career, and my image drove me to always appear as if I had it all together. Everything had to be perfect. All the time. Now that

I think back on it, I must have been pretty unbearable at times to those who had to live with me (thank God for family . . . they're still around). But there's nothing like living Murphy's Law to humble you.

Over the past few years, I have faced a number of challenges—financial, personal, professional, and material—that have forced me to confront issues I thought I had dealt with long ago. Only to find out that I had just scratched the surface of what I have now come to understand were insecurities and doubts that were still plaguing me from childhood.

Sometimes insecurity can manifest itself in very subtle ways, while other times it's more obvious. For me, it reared its ugly head in the form of using material things to reflect to the world that I was worthy. The funny thing is, I have never thought of myself as materialistic. I wasn't one to lose my mind over the latest designer bag or brand name shoes. Nope, my Maama taught me how to be frugal and so I've always looked for a great bargain without sacrificing quality. But, I also always made sure that whatever I did buy reflected the fact that I was doing pretty well, thank you.

So what happens when you can no longer afford to keep up appearances? Some people die trying. Me? At the point when things got really tight, and my business that I had run successfully for six years had slowed to a snail's limp (the poor thing was on crutches!), God told me to just let it all go. Let go of feeling like I'm not allowed to make a mistake. Let go of thinking I can't ask for help. Let go of putting on a happy face to mask my inner turmoil. Let go of the need to prove that I am worthy by using material things to define my worth. Let. It. Go. Let go of relationships that were becoming toxic. Let go of the home I had invested so much in. Let go of having to be strong—all the time. And I have to say, it was quite freeing. When I finally humbled myself enough to give myself permission to be human, I asked myself why it had taken me so long.

I can now say that I am grateful for those challenges I

experienced. Without them, I would never have been forced to really look myself in the eye and admit that my determination to keep on my "success" mask was what had caused me to make decisions that landed me where I was: unhappy, unsatisfied, and extremely uncomfortable. As I shined the flashlight on my internal gremlins, I recognized the patterns that had played out over my life while I tried to show the world I could be bad all by myself. I started identifying the different masks I had worn throughout my life.

The following is a list of masks many of us wear to keep from allowing others to see how human we really are. Which ones do you identify with?

TYPES OF MASKS WE WEAR

- **Success:** The expensive car, the brand name clothing, the six-figure job. All that bling keeps you at a safe distance from the lack of self-worth you mask with material things.

- **Apathy:** You've learned that when you care too much, you get hurt, so instead you act like you couldn't care less about anything. Truth is, you secretly want to allow the love that's inside to come out, but you're too afraid of what that would mean for your self-preservation.

- **Superwoman:** You're da woman! Don't need any help and can do it all by yourself. Or die trying.

- **Happy-Go-Lucky:** People love being around you because you're always smiling. Your husband is perfect. Your children are perfect. Your life is perfect. Nothing is ever wrong. On the outside.

- **DIVA (in all CAPS):** Don't let anyone try to tell you anything. You are a diva all the way and have the high-maintenance attitude to prove it. Anyone who wants the honor of your company has got to pay (dearly) to play. How else will you know how important you are?

- **Large-and-in-Charge:** Your pantsuit should really be a suit of armor. Always in charge, you never let anyone see weakness or vulnerability.

- **Helpless:** There is almost nothing you *can* do by yourself. Whining is your calling card. You're the opposite of Superwoman, but use your feigned helplessness to manipulate.

- **Know-It-All:** God forbid there's anything you don't know the answer to. Pity the person who tries to reason with you. You use your imagined omniscience to keep your internal feelings of inferiority from showing externally.

- **Don't Mess With Me:** You don't know anything about showing a softer side. What's that? You've learned that you have to steamroll people in order to get what you want, including love. How's that working for you?

- **Irresistible**: Acting cute has gotten you this far. Why ruin things by allowing your intelligence to let people know there's more to you than a pretty face and a flirtatious smile?

- **Networker:** You collect business cards like candy. The more contacts you have in your cell phone, Twitter account, and on Facebook, the more you'll believe that people really like you—especially if they're "important." But the real question is, do you like yourself?

- **Manipulator:** Afraid that people won't like you enough to help you or love you just because, you use manipulation as a way to keep others from leaving you.

- **Yes-Woman:** You believe that being needed by others—all the time—is the ultimate ego boost. So anyone who ever needs anything (whether at 3:15 p.m. or 3:15 a.m.) can call on you because you never say "no." Never mind whether or not you feel resentful. You're just being of service. No?

Many of us have been taught that appearances are everything: your hair has to look a certain way; you can't leave your house without makeup; your clothes have to be a certain brand. For a number of us, we don't even realize we're wearing a mask. The masks we wear ensure that the world never gets to know what really takes place inside of our heads and our hearts. Our doubts, our fears, our insecurities, our dysfunctional families, the things we don't like about ourselves—they all help keep our masks firmly in place. Keep in mind, however, that while you're expending all this energy holding on tightly to your mask, you're probably not fooling as many people as you think.

Here's a simple way to figure out if you're wearing a mask. Is the image you portray to the outside world in sync with who you are when you're alone? Regardless of the circle of people you are with at any given time, do you feel comfortable allowing the real you to shine through? Are you afraid to show your vulnerability because you've been taught that that's weak? Keep in mind that this is different from having to carry yourself a certain way at your day job (e.g., law enforcement, doctor, lawyer, etc.). There are times when you have to maintain a certain decorum because of the work that you do. But once you're off the clock, if you're still not able to just be yourself, then it's time to begin chipping away at that veneer. Because until you are able to bring your authentic self to the table, you will never really be able to enjoy the feast that is your life. You'll be too busy worrying about what everyone else is thinking about what's on your plate.

If you've ever dated someone you didn't see a future with, but who fit in with everyone else's image of who you should be with; taken on a mortgage you couldn't afford so you could keep up a certain image; paid for a weave that cost more than your car payment (which you were behind on); taken on a certain persona in public that you dreaded but thought necessary for acceptance; refused to leave your house without makeup; or, put on a smile for the world, when inside all you felt was confusion, turmoil, and sadness, then it's time for us to do some work.

You're exhausted, aren't you? It's tiring trying to keep up with an image that doesn't speak to who you really are or want to be. In my own journey of peeling away the layers of masks I have worn throughout my life, I had several come-to-Jesus meetings with Jesus himself (that's when you *know* it's serious). Those talks were invaluable. They revealed some really important truths. One of the most important being that, in the past, whenever I bought nice things for myself, it was because I was using them to mask what I thought were my inadequacies—not simply because, as a child of God and the daughter of a King, I deserved the best.

I now understand that I am valuable. What I bring to the table is valuable, and I no longer feel like I have anything to prove to anyone but myself. I am because I am. I am because He is. Now when I buy or do nice things for myself, it will just be because I love myself enough to know I deserve them. Period. The same goes for everything else in my life. I expect the best because I deserve it. Success will no longer be about proving anything to anyone. It will now be because it brings me joy, glorifies God, and will help me serve the world better.

Keep this in mind whenever you find yourself slipping back to wearing one of your masks:

"I am so valuable that Jesus lay down his life for me. By believing, thinking, or acting like I am less than what He said I am—which is a child of the most High God—I am dishonoring Him and the sacrifice He made for me."

What a powerful revelation that was for me! Understanding this has made it much easier for me to let go of and accept certain things in my life. In fact, understanding what it meant to remove my mask(s) and stand in my truth is what has allowed me to share my many lessons with you throughout this book.

TWEET THIS! @WhoseShoesBook
I am perfectly powerful in my imperfection.
#whoseshoes

Because I am learning to embrace my imperfections, I am no longer as afraid of making a mistake as I used to be. I don't feel the pressure to be seen at the right event with the right people in the right photo op. I no longer worry so much about external material things reflecting who I want people to think I am. Instead, I am much more focused on continuing to build the internal, so that it can truly reflect who I am and what I want to attract into my life. And you know those neighbors, the Joneses, who I was way too busy trying to keep up with? I moved out of their neighborhood into one that has all the amenities I need for this next chapter of my life. It's much closer to where I want to be.

I'm not going to lie to you. Taking off your mask is *hard*. Any time you force yourself out of your comfort zone, it's going to be hard. But as you begin to tear down those walls, you'll find freedom. Freedom to be who you really are. Freedom to connect with others on a deeper level. Freedom to love and allow yourself to be vulnerable, even when there is the possibility of being hurt. Because even if you get hurt, you'll be able to remember that you've survived and you've always come out on the other side stronger and wiser. And you'll begin to attract others to your light. So many of us are tired of the pretending and the profiling. Our souls long to connect with others on a deeper, spiritual level, but more often than not, that connection is blocked by our inability or unwillingness to be authentic.

FINDING YOUR SHOES

So how in the world do you go about chipping away at that mask? It starts with figuring out where it came from. Grab your journal and pen so you can begin writing your reflections.

1. Identify.
Answer the following questions:

- Where did you learn that wearing a mask was necessary for survival or success?

- Were you teased about your looks when you were younger and now overcompensate for that as an adult by having to look together all the time? Describe those incidents and how they made you feel.

- Were you hurt deeply by someone you cared about, forcing you to put on your anti-vulnerability mask so you didn't get hurt again? Can you forgive them in order to free your soul from continuing to be a prisoner of unforgiveness? What would that feel like to you?

Are you beginning to see the connection between your current choices and behaviors, and any unresolved issues or pain you may still be hanging on to from your past? I'm here to tell you that those masks are heavy, burdensome, and hard to carry around all the time. But to deal with a problem, you have to first get to its root. Once you've identified where your mask came from, it's time to determine what it's costing you. Health? Finances? Unconditional love? Deeper relationships? A closer relationship with God? Your sanity? Personal growth? Fulfillment? Define the price you are paying to hold on to that mask, and then decide if the things it's costing you are more important than the illusion of safety it provides.

2. Affirm.

Here are some personal affirmations that have helped me, and which can help you begin peeling back those false layers to reveal the real you:

- Money does not define who I am.

- I am more than my possessions. (As they say, you don't ever see a hearse towing a U-Haul truck behind it.)

- My worth comes from the Divinity that lies within.

- I am fearfully and wonderfully made. (Psalm 139:14)

- I have all that I need to become the person that I want.

- The light that shines from within me is more attractive than the expensive, shiny things that surround me.

- By allowing myself to be vulnerable, I open the door to more meaningful relationships.

- I am perfect in my imperfection.

- I don't need awards or recognition to know that my life and my work have value.

- I am worthy of love, respect, and success (however you define it) because of who I am, not what I have.

- A mistake doesn't mean I'm horrible; it just means I'm human.

You can come up with your own affirmations to help you realize that what you cultivate internally will be what you exude externally. Make it a daily habit to reaffirm the real you every day. And keep in mind, most people are savvy enough to spot a fake. Instead of living in fear of being "found out," just be (the real) you!

3. Address.

Now the work begins: you have to commit to the change. Part of the commitment may require you to make amends or ask forgiveness for those things you may have done or said to hurt others in a desperate attempt to cling to your own mask for dear life. I had to do this with one colleague in particular when I came to this realization.

When I was just starting out in my career, I didn't know as much about empathy and authenticity as I do now, and, decided to tell her about herself. I thought I was doing her a favor by letting her know what all our other colleagues were saying about her inappropriate behavior at work. Instead, I chipped away at her already low self-esteem to aid in keeping my own mask, and my own insecurities, in place. A few years later, when I realized how self-righteous I had been, I took her out to lunch and apologized for that incident. She was gracious enough to accept my apology and thank me for my honesty and willingness to admit my wrong. My spirit felt much lighter, and I was a better person for it.

Who do you have in your life that you've hurt or disrespected while wearing one of your masks—knowingly or unknowingly? Write down the names of all those people who you need to ask for their forgiveness (and even those you need to forgive), and begin the work of breaking the chains of unforgiveness that keep your mask in place. This doesn't mean that you go through your phone book and call up every single person you've ever hurt in your life (with some people, you can pray for their forgiveness at a distance); however, you should let your spirit be your guide to know who you need to make amends with in order to be freed from your past.

Keep in mind that you may have hurt some people so deeply that they may not be willing or ready to grant you the forgiveness you seek. Be prepared for that. Everyone takes their own time to process different situations. If that happens, then know that as long as you're doing it with the right intentions, you don't have to stay stuck, even if they do. Keep moving. Keep growing. Keep transforming.

2 THE DEFINITION OF INSANITY
CHRISTINE

The statistics on sanity are that one out of every four people is suffering from mental illness. Look at your three best friends. If they're okay, then it's you. —Rita Mae Brown

Webster's definition of insanity is, "the state of being seriously mentally ill; madness." The more modern definition of insanity is, "doing the same thing over and over again and expecting different results." I'd agree that equals madness, wouldn't you? We've all done it. Most of the time, we continue to do the same thing because it's comfortable or because we think if we just continue to do it, it'll get better. How's that working for you? Chances are, it's not. And only when you decide to finally admit it to yourself, will you be able to take the necessary steps to make that needed change.

I will never forget my experience at what I thought was my dream job. It was at least forty minutes closer to home than my previous job; paid more money; offered free parking, meals, and dry cleaning; and seriously, it was fun! I just knew I'd hit the jackpot. For the first time in a really long time, I absolutely loved going to work each and every day. I mean, who wouldn't? It was red carpet treatment. We were treated like stars, at least in the beginning.

But sometime after the first year, things took a turn for the worse.

There was a major layoff almost exactly a year after I started working there. Taking into consideration that it was also right before the recession hit in 2009, I guess I shouldn't have found it odd that 90% of those who were terminated were African Americans in upper-level management. No, it wasn't strange that some of them were told their positions were no longer needed and were being eliminated because of financial reasons, only to have those same positions filled weeks later by their white counterparts. Nope, not too strange at all.

Have you ever seen the writing on the wall but fooled yourself into believing that it was all in your head? Or that even though it was happening to someone else right before your eyes, there was no way it could or would happen to you? Well, this is exactly how my mind was working at that time. I saw so much that was unethical happening all around me, but I was in denial that I would ever have to confront it myself. Besides, not only was I great at what I did, I also worked in Human Resources. We were fair and played by the rules. Not!

I think one of the reasons it took me a while to accept the inevitable was the fact that I loved my job so much. I have had two supervisors in my corporate career that were absolutely phenomenal. They were the type of managers who encouraged and motivated me to learn more. They treated me like the leader I was, and if I made mistakes, they worked with me, instead of against me (read: instead of throwing me under the bus) to help resolve them. I knew that if I ever had any concern or issue I needed to raise, I could go to them in confidence and trust that they would address the problem to the best of their abilities.

It's hard to go from this type of relationship with my boss, to the one I had with David (not his real name, but the one we'll use for the purpose of this book). David was a micro-manager. I appreciate feedback and take direction well, but what I can't tolerate is someone breathing down my neck and asking how an assignment is going five minutes after they've given it to me. I also couldn't stomach his incessant need to have meetings about meetings. I know some of you can feel me on this one. You're given a project, but then can never get to it because you have five meetings a day to talk about the project. Well, that was my reality. But remember, this was my "dream job." As long as I pushed through this, it would eventually get better.

It was during this time, with the change in leadership across the company, that I became pregnant with my second child. Since I worked all the way through my pregnancy with my first, I felt that I would be able to do it again with my second. Only this time it was slightly different. This time I was dealing with a boss whom I didn't get along with and a job that was becoming increasingly stressful. There were a number of things taking place around me that I didn't agree with, but again, I just knew it was going to get better. I kept hearing that voice telling me that I needed to start thinking about my next move. I ignored it because, for me, this was my next move. As we all know, when we continue to do what we know we shouldn't, it will eventually backfire. Remember that definition of insanity we talked about?

By my eighth month of pregnancy, the stress had become unbearable. It wasn't even my heavy workload that was stressing me out. Instead, it was dealing with my manager. By this time, I had trouble sleeping at night, and felt sick at just the thought of going in to work. I could feel myself immediately tense up anytime my boss would pass by or pop his head in my office. I knew that he was never just stopping in to say "hi," but instead wanted a report on what I was working on. It got to the point where it was affecting my ability to do my job efficiently because I kept second-guessing myself and going back to triple-check all of my work (even when I knew it was right). If you've ever had to deal with a bully of a manager on the job, then you know what I'm talking about. While I thought I could handle the stress until it was time for me to go out on maternity leave, my doctor thought it best that I be put on bed rest for the last month of my pregnancy.

During my time on leave, that voice started talking to me again. "Are you sure you should be going back to this job? You really should take this time to look for other opportunities because things aren't going to get any better." But I was convinced that all I needed was a little break from it all. Once I'd had some time to breathe and my hormones had calmed down, everything would go back to what it was when I had first started working there. I was sure of it! Oh, but I was so very wrong.

Even after my boss had been terminated, things at work didn't improve as I had hoped. Fast forward two years later. David was replaced by another bully boss (just when I thought things couldn't get any worse), and I was pregnant with my third child. I was still in the same position, at the same office and dealing with the same shenanigans. Insane, right? At the time, I didn't think so, but looking back now, I just shake my head. There was really no one else to blame but myself.

I was so stressed and exhausted by the end of my first trimester that I had constant migraines, and can't remember a day when I didn't cry from the stress of it all. I remember getting my very first disciplinary action—ever. It's one thing when you see something coming and can brace yourself, but totally another when you get knocked off your feet from something that snuck up behind you. And that's exactly what happened. Not only did it come as a surprise, but it was given to me by someone who was a contractor and had been on the job for less than six weeks. With the write-up, also came an ultimatum: either I could choose to put in for a transfer to a different position (and department), or stay in my current position and risk losing my job (not in those exact words, but that was the message that rang loud and clear). So what would you do?

At this point, that voice started talking to me again. The writing was on the wall, and it was time for me to plan my exit. But surely, God wasn't telling me to just leave. No, I thought He wanted me to hang in there until it was time to go out on maternity leave—or at least that's what I kept telling myself until it was believable. We were expecting baby number three. How in the world were we going to survive on only one income? I just had to get through the next six months and then everything would be okay.

I kept hearing that voice telling me to leave, so I started looking for another job (and quickly before my baby bump started expanding). I put in some applications and was called in for three different management interviews. For one in particular, I was called back twice and met with at least eight different people (including the vice president). I was convinced that this was the job God had lined up for me to take me out of my misery! I kept waiting for the offer . . . and waiting. It never came. Instead, I continued pursuing other opportunities, and hanging on to a job that was affecting my health and that of my unborn child. I just needed to make it to maternity leave.

Then one day, I opened up my e-mail to find an invitation to attend a seminar entitled "Dare to Live Your Dreams." It promised to deliver on helping you find your purpose and figure out what was keeping you stuck. I will never forget when the instructor got on the topic of people in the room who were miserable, unhappy, and stressed in their current employment situations. He said, "God will put you in a holy discontent to get you out of certain situations." This one sentence nearly knocked me off my pregnant feet (thank goodness I was sitting down). I distinctly remember my eyes welling up with tears because, at that moment, I knew without a shadow of a doubt that God was talking directly to me, through the instructor.

Have you ever been so uneasy, uncomfortable, and stressed in a job or situation that you were just restless? Have you ever felt like fleeing from those situations, only to force yourself to stay out of obligation or fear that you don't have a choice? Well, I did just that because I thought it was my only choice at the time. See, with my first pregnancy at this job, things were bad, and I knew then I should've left. But I stayed out of fear and convenience. Even after God put me in a holy discontent, it took me another couple of months to get up the courage to leave my job.

All the while, my husband kept telling me to leave. He saw how it was affecting my mentality and my attitude with him and the kids. For someone who is genuinely a happy person, I was far from it at this point. Instead of dealing with and talking about my issues at work, I was taking my frustrations out on my family. I was frazzled, frustrated, short-tempered, and probably not an ounce of fun to be around. It wasn't cute. When you're stressed and unhappy, it affects everyone around you, including yourself. I learned this the hard way.

Instead of sleeping, I would spend the night tossing and turning, and it had nothing to do with being uncomfortable with my pregnancy. I was full of anxiety, which was affecting my mentality. But most importantly, it was affecting my health and that of my unborn child. At just five and a half months pregnant, I was experiencing Braxton Hicks contractions.

How has your insanity affected your relationships? Chances are, you may be so deep into your own insanity that you don't even realize you're neglecting those closest to you. I was so wrapped up with my drama at work that I didn't even realize I had been taking it out on my husband and children. After spending a week at home (under my doctor's orders), all of my symptoms vanished. I didn't have any trouble sleeping at all that week, and I didn't experience even one Braxton Hicks during that time. That's when I knew I had to make that final choice.

What I realized a year after I left my last corporate job, was that:

TWEET THIS! @WhoseShoesBook
God had to get me away from the distractions in order for me to clearly see my purpose. #whoseshoes

And my purpose had nothing to do with continuing to climb the corporate ladder. I will never forget when I got that confirmation from God. The year I left my job, was the same year my husband's overtime pay was almost exactly what my annual salary would've been. To add icing to the cake, we received our first ever five-digit tax return that year as well. I say this, not to brag, but to underscore the fact that God was reminding me that as long as I continued putting my faith and trust in Him, He would in turn take care of me and my loved ones. We have not missed my corporate paycheck since.

Instead, we have been abundantly blessed, and ever since, I've been stepping out on faith. Through this process, I learned that everything happens in God's timing (as cliché as that might sound). But more importantly, I learned that I couldn't allow fear to keep me from moving in the direction that He was moving me. No matter the situation, the fear will never go away until we face it head on. Walking out on my job was one of the scariest things I have ever done, but looking back, it's been the most rewarding because I was able to find my purpose and start my own business (more on Moms 'N Charge a little later).

FINDING YOUR SHOES

Grab your journal and begin writing down answers to the following in order to uncover the reasons you're staying stuck:

1. Identify.
What or who are you allowing to keep you stuck?
Example: Saying "yes" to every request made of me.

2. Determine the cost.
What are those distractions costing you?
Example: Taking time away from what I want to accomplish.

3. Take decisive action.

What three changes can you make today to begin to eliminate your distractions, and things you tolerate which you shouldn't?

4. Create your own community.

Having an accountability partner or small group can be a powerful thing in moving you forward with your goals. Align yourself with people who are where you want to be, or going where you want to go.

3 LISTENING TO THAT STILL, SMALL VOICE
JULIAN

Sometimes making that next bold move requires listening to that still, small voice. —Julian B. Kiganda

I'm going to keep it real (and hope that my pastor doesn't read this book), and admit that those long Sunday sermons are often when my mind leaves the service and takes a stroll around my mental neighborhood. It's not because I don't love the Lord and value His Word; on the contrary, I get my "spiritual food" for the week from fellowshipping with other believers. It's just that, sometimes, that's the longest stretch of time in the entire week that I am forced to be still. But my pastor's giving a forty-five-minute sermon (forty-five minutes is a long time in a Catholic church when you're used to the entire service taking an hour) is no excuse for not focusing my energies where they should be when I'm in church—on my relationship with God.

No matter where you worship, if you are to lead a purpose-driven life, your relationship with your Creator needs to be a priority. That is something I thank my parents for. They raised all seven (yes, seven) of us with strong spiritual values that we didn't truly "get" until we were older. For many years, I went through the motions of going to church out of obligation, not knowing what a gift I had in knowing the Lord.

As I got older, I took the initiative to understand what it really meant to have a personal relationship with God, which had less to do with religion and everything to do with feeding and connecting with my soul. Religion was the tool I used to make that connection. This makes me think of Iyanla Vanzant's definition of the soul: "The fingerprint of God that becomes a physical body."

How easily we forget that we are divine beings! What if we were to tap into that part of ourselves more often? What if we took the time to *be still* so that we could hear what our souls were trying to tell us. There are so many times I wish I had listened to that still, small voice before making life-altering decisions.

I remember several years ago when I decided to try online dating after having been divorced for some time. A girlfriend of mine and I were tired of the nightclub scene and figured we'd have as good a chance as any at finding "Mr. Right" in cyberspace. I have nothing against online dating—actually, yeah, I do. I'm sure it's worked for a number of people, but after this one "memorable" experience, I decided that probably wasn't where my husband was going to surface.

It was the summer of 2007 and my first foray into cyber-dating. It didn't take long to realize that there were some dudes with real issues on the Internet. I understand that we all have issues to some degree, but I'm talking about having more issues than *Sports Illustrated* (I've always wanted to say that!). After sifting through all of what I thought were the duds, I came across one guy who had reached out to me with two simple words: "Hi Beautiful."

OMG!!! He called me beautiful! And then I checked out his profile. For the sake of anonymity, I'll call him Mark. Mark seemed like a dream. He was an IT professional (translate: made good money), loved to travel (so did I!), and had a daughter (so did I!). From his profile, he seemed like a real gentleman—but wait, there was more. *He wrote poetry*. The man wrote poetry. And he had posted one of his poems on his profile. I mean, how much more romantic could you get than that?

Wow. Just wow.

I took one more look at his profile picture before I decided to respond, and then I paused. He was wearing glasses, but I could still make out his eyes, which were green. They say that the eyes are the window to the soul. When I looked at his, I thought I heard mini-alarm bells ringing, but it couldn't be. He looked only slightly crazy. Why and how could I get warning signals from a man who wrote *poetry* about *love*. I squashed it and responded to his message. It was probably just nervous jitters anyway.

And so it went for a couple of days: back and forth on instant messaging through the dating service, giving details here and there about who we were. Then we finally exchanged numbers. The day Mark called, I was away from the phone and instead found his voicemail. Darn! Twenty minutes later, I caught my breath, counted to thirty, and called him back. We talked for only a few minutes because he was on his way to meet with a client, but it was long enough for us to set up a first date.

It turned out to be more of a rendezvous than a date, as Mark fit me in between client meetings. We agreed to meet at a coffee shop in a nearby mall. So you know how we females do; I primped and prepped and took three hours to look casual, but cute. I didn't want him to think I had done all that just for him. Even though I had.

As I headed to the mall, I was excited about meeting this poet in person. Anticipation had my heart beating out of control. Get it together, Ju. My phone rang. It was him. I picked up.

"Hello?"

"Hi, Julian, how are you? It's Mark."

"Hi, Mark, I'm good."

"Well, I just wanted to let you know that I'm here. I'm wearing jeans and a tan polo shirt."

"Okay, I'll be there in a couple of minutes," I said, as I continued walking towards our meeting spot. Here went nothing. As I rounded the corner and spotted him in the food court, it took everything in me not to react. Negatively.

The man looked like he had dodged an iron—on purpose. He certainly hadn't made any attempt to "dress to impress." He also looked better online than in person (isn't that almost always the case?). Not that he was bad-looking, but his clothes certainly didn't help. Yeah, this was going to be an extremely brief encounter. I began plotting my escape, but outwardly, I put on a smile and went to say hello. After all, I was raised with proper manners.

Although I was ready to write him off, he was quite the charmer. I had to admit, I enjoyed our conversation. He may not have been the most polished guy I had ever met, but he made me laugh and showed genuine interest in me. He was starting to look better and better. And did I mention he was a *poet*? During that initial meeting, I asked him a question about his family, and he froze; a brief, but intense flash of anger lit up his eyes. And then it disappeared just as quickly as it came. But something in me was uneasy about his reaction. I ignored it. I mean, the man wrote poetry—about love.

Over the course of the next month, Mark and I got to know each other and went on several dates. I swear he was everything I thought I wanted in a guy (as long as I ignored his apparent aversion to an iron, minor outbursts of anger here and there, and that still, small voice that was trying to tell me something wasn't quite right). He opened doors, pulled out my chair, paid for everything, complimented me incessantly, and told me every single thing I wanted to hear. Everything. He even gave me a signed copy of a book of poetry he had written and self-published. Eventually, he told me he wanted to marry me and would do whatever it took to prove that I was the woman he wanted to spend the rest of his life with. And imagine, it had only taken him four weeks to realize that. Who said God didn't answer prayers?

For several weeks, I was on cloud nine—until his true colors started coming out. Note that none of my siblings had met him yet (mistake); however, a couple of my girlfriends who had, told me that they didn't like the way he talked to me. That should have been a clue, right? But instead, I made excuses for him and smoothed over the negative with all of the positive that I could find.

Eventually, the wheels started coming off slowly, but surely. Mark started taking days to return my calls. Even after he claimed he'd deleted his profile from the dating site we had met on, because he had finally found "the woman of his dreams," I found out that he was still quite active on the site. When we did talk, he found reasons to pick an argument. Then that flash of anger I had seen on our first date became more prevalent, and he just became mean and disparaging.

I remember one conversation we had during which I questioned him about why he hadn't returned my calls. He became really angry and told me that if I wasn't careful, I would regret being "all up in his business" and would cause some real damage to our relationship. He also became noticeably angry whenever I told him that he had a choice in the way he reacted to situations. Nothing was ever his fault because the whole world was against him. Another red flag I ignored was the fact that he was estranged from his entire family (including his young daughter and her mother) because of a falling-out he'd had with all of them—again, not his fault. Had I paid more attention to how he spoke negatively about the women in his life, I would have gotten a clue as to how he would eventually treat me. Although I never felt like I was in any danger when we were together, his erratic and angry outbursts during our phone conversations were a sign of what our relationship could become. Where had the romantic poet disappeared to?

When I recognized that his Jekyll-and-Hyde personality was something that I was not willing to put up with, I decided to send him a break-up e-mail—secretly hoping that he would realize what an amazing woman he was giving up and come to his senses. His response to my e-mail left no room for doubt that the dream guy had revealed himself to be the person he *really* was instead of what I had wanted him to be. In one simple sentence, he left as quickly as he had come into my life: "If that's what you want, I wish you the best in life." End of story.

Luckily for me, I was able to break it off in time to avoid the relationship becoming any more abusive than it already was. But it was still hard because, in my mind, I had started planning a future with this guy the moment I read his poetry. When I finally got over my severely bruised ego and realized that I had dodged a bullet, I was able to accept the lessons I was meant to learn from this incident, not the least of which were the following:

1. Trust your intuition. Initially, I would have never considered a relationship with him because of the way he presented himself, but then I read the poetry and fell in love with the *idea* and the *ideal* of him—not the actual person.

2. Stop compromising. Stop settling. Stop searching. Your time will come when you're ready, and when it's right. Relax and continue having fun and living your life.

3. Love is patient. The man who is meant for you will know that he has to work for you and work to keep you. He will respect and be compatible with your spiritual and moral beliefs. Accept no less than that.

4. Pay attention to the way a person lives. Their hygiene, their speech, how they talk about other people—those are all good indicators of their character and where they are spiritually.

5. Stop being disobedient when the Spirit is trying to get your attention. I should have paid closer attention to my first reaction to

his online picture. The eyes are truly the window to the soul.

6. Steer clear of insecure, negative people.

7. If someone is always complaining about everyone else and how the whole world is against them, then something's wrong. This means that they don't take responsibility for anything. Run. Fast.

8. Pay attention to the relationship that a man (or a woman) has with his family—especially how he treats and speaks to his mother, as well as how he talks about other women. That is a huge clue as to how he's going to eventually treat, and talk about you.

9. Don't be so sure of yourself that you don't take other people's opinions or warnings into consideration. They might be the voice of the Holy Spirit.

10. There's no need to rush anything, especially relationships; if it's part of God's plan, it will be, no matter what. Remember, love is patient.

TWEET THIS! @WhoseShoesBook
Don't be afraid to make mistakes. Sometimes, they're the best way to learn a lifelong lesson. #whoseshoes

TWEET THIS! @WhoseShoesBook
Remember that hurting people hurt people. It has nothing to do with you. #whoseshoes

I could have saved myself six weeks of heartache had I just listened to that warning bell that rang the first time I saw Mark's profile picture online.

Be honest with yourself. How many times have you heard a voice, your gut, the Spirit—whatever you want to call it—tell you not to do whatever it was you were about to do? Or maybe that voice has tried to direct you to a decision or an action that you've been putting off or avoiding. What has it cost you not to listen to that voice?

That online dating incident was only one example of the many times I have ignored that voice I call the Holy Spirit. Why do we do that? Why do we ignore that alarm bell that goes off when we are about to make a decision that could alter the course of our lives?

I've come to understand that it's because we don't trust ourselves enough to know what's best for us. We've grown up being told how to act, what to do, what to wear, who to like, what to like—so much so that our own voice, our intuition, has been drowned out and has yielded to the world's voice. And yet, true joy and success can only come when you follow that voice, that call that God has placed on your heart to guide you on your path. So the question is, how do you find that voice and learn to tune into it more often?

FINDING YOUR SHOES

It's time to pull out your journal and put pen to paper. Follow these three steps to put you on the path to following your inner voice and transforming your life into what you have always envisioned:

1. Clear the clutter.

Imagine being at a sports game with fans yelling all around you while you try to have a deep, life-changing conversation with your best friend, who's sitting right next to you. Can you really focus on your conversation in the midst of all this noise? Well, the reality is, that's what many of us try to do on a regular basis whenever we try to think through major decisions. But instead of being all around us, the clutter usually starts in the mind and then manifests itself outwardly.

Often, we're comfortable in the clutter. That means that we don't have to deal with the real mess that lies beneath. But I know for sure that you can't have peace of mind until you clear the clutter in your mind *and* in your surroundings. That might mean different things to different people, but start with this:

In your journal, begin to put on paper every single thing that you're worried about, excited about, thinking about, planning on doing, don't want to do, and that is just taking up space in your head. *Do not* censor anything that comes out. Think of this as "spring cleaning" for your mind. This may take some time, but give yourself a limit of thirty minutes to get it all down. When you finish, take a deep breath, and exhale. You've taken the first step to making room in your mind for what you really want.

Next, you're going to review your list and highlight only the things that you: a) have control over and absolutely *have* to do in order to reach your goals; and b) are truly passionate about. If you have more than five things highlighted, continue editing; otherwise, you will feel overwhelmed trying to do everything at once. Everything else can wait. I promise you, the world will not end if you don't get to it right now.

Now you need to prioritize and set deadlines for each of those items and put together a plan to realize them. It doesn't need to be complicated, but it should be realistic so that you don't become defeated if for some reason you don't reach your first milestone. You've got to put it in your mind that quitting is not an option. Let your inner voice guide you on your next move.

2. Allow your opinion to be the most important one.

There's nothing wrong with getting feedback from people whom you trust about a decision you are about to make; however, there comes a time when you have to stop looking for approval and validation from others. You have to trust that the same God who created you, already implanted the answers in your soul. You just need to clear out your connection to Him, so you can hear His voice. When you trust yourself, you no longer say that you don't know what you want. I believe that we always know what we want. We're just too afraid to admit it, or too confused by everyone else's ideas and opinions of what we should want, to be able to voice it.

You have to get to the point where you get real with yourself and decide that—as uncomfortable as it may be at first—you are no longer going to allow that still, small (sometimes loud) voice to be drowned out by everyone else. Practice making your opinion the one that matters, regardless of who may get offended. This doesn't mean that you become disrespectful towards others, but it *does* mean that for the issues that most affect your ability to live your life on purpose, your voice should drown out everyone else's. This is a muscle that will need to be exercised in order to become stronger, so as you develop it, know that it's a process. And be okay with learning on the job. Don't forget to pat yourself on the back each time you take a baby step in the right direction. Celebrate your success every step of the way.

3. Pray. Surrender. And then let it go.

This is the most important step for any type of transformation, especially the part where you're trying to hone in on your inner voice—your spirit—to guide you through the process. Our parents have always stressed to my siblings and me the importance of prayer and trusting God, but I wasn't sure what that really meant when I was younger. Then I grew up and began to understand that prayer is more than just asking God for favors and giving Him my take-out order; it's about having a two-way conversation, during which I listen more than I talk. As they say, that's why we are given two ears and only one mouth. God is always speaking to us; sometimes it's that inner voice, sometimes it's through other people, and sometimes it's through circumstances. But unless we're willing to be still and listen as we pray and meditate, we can easily miss that message.

As you try to figure out your life and become the person you know you were meant to be, prayer is your pathway to purpose and the spark that will ignite your passion. Just know, that if you're a typical type A+++ like me (and even if you're not), the most difficult part of prayer is surrender. Because as human beings, we want to control the outcome and the timing. Once you've done your part, you have to let God do His.

TWEET THIS! @WhoseShoesBook
Pray, or worry–you can't do both faithfully.
#whoseshoes

Mastering the art of surrender will free you from feeling like you have to be in control of everything. And it will teach you that learning to trust yourself is the ultimate prayer to the Divine that lives within.

4 WHERE DID SELF-LOVE GO WRONG?

CHRISTINE

Love yourself . . . enough to take the actions required for your happiness . . . enough to cut yourself loose from the drama-filled past . . . enough to set a high standard for relationships . . . enough to forgive yourself . . . enough to move on. —Dr. Steve Maraboli

The term "self-love" gets tossed around so frequently these days that people don't really understand the importance of it. It influences everyday decisions you make and the image you project to other people. What image do you want to reflect to the world? People will respond to what you express on the outside. Chances are, if you express doubt, low self-esteem, or uncertainty, you will get those same things in return. If you don't believe in yourself, how can you convince others to believe in you? Self-love is something you cultivate, resulting from conscious actions you take.

When someone talks to you about falling in love, does the thought of falling in love with yourself ever cross your mind? The truth of the matter is that you can't reach your full potential until you've learned to truly FLY: First Love Yourself. How do you treat yourself when no one is watching? How do you treat yourself when all eyes are on you? If there's one thing I've learned over the last few years, it's the importance of self-love. And if it's not something that was embedded into your spirit from a young age, it can be a very hard thing to understand and put into practice.

Growing up in our African household, the word "love" was never really heard or expressed to us. Our parents hardly ever told us they loved us, and as siblings, we definitely never spoke those words to one another (it was just something we were supposed to know and understand through actions). Our parents always instilled in us the importance of doing well in school and making sure we were doing what we were supposed to be doing. But telling us how beautiful or smart we were, or how much they loved us wasn't a part of their parenting philosophy. It just wasn't something they had grown up with themselves. So what I ended up lacking was self-confidence. What I ended up lacking for many years, even into adulthood, was self-love. What I ended up lacking was the ability to see myself as smart, beautiful, and worthy of true love.

It was hard enough to grow up as an African in America. Yes, I was born in Washington, DC, and raised in the suburbs of Montgomery County, MD, but as far as my parents were concerned, I was all African. I remember resenting my African heritage at times, especially during my elementary and middle school years. It's one thing to always be the tallest, but another when you're also the darkest (many times the only Black) and sometimes skinniest person in the classroom. I always felt like I had two identities: Chrissy, the Ugandan-American when she was at home and amongst family members, and Christine, the all-American girl (or so she tried to be) as soon as she stepped foot outside the house with her friends.

My family knew my middle name as Nakabuye (yeah, try that one out), but anytime someone at school asked me what my middle name was, it was always Nancy, or I just didn't have one (depending on who was asking and how I was feeling that day). And forget about how I always hated the start of a new school year with a new teacher when it was time to do roll call. My last name, Kiganda, always got butchered and usually garnered several stares and giggles.

I was never the most popular, and felt like I was far from the prettiest girl, in any of my classes. I will never forget being in the sixth grade when I had one of my first experiences with my self-image and self-love truly being crushed. A close girlfriend of mine at the time (let's call her Diane), had told me about her cousin and showed me a picture of him. I thought he was cute (we'll call him James), and she had told him about me. So he was interested in seeing a picture of me, which I didn't know at the time. That year I had taken what I knew was a really horrible school picture, and I decided to take it over during the make-up session.

Well, Diane hadn't received my new picture, so she gave him my "ugly" Christine picture. I distinctly remember her telling me, "I showed James your picture, and he is not interested in going out with you." That was the terminology we used back in the day. It was the tone in her voice and the next thing she said that made me want to curl up and cry my eyes out. "He didn't like the picture."

If someone who hadn't even met me thought I was ugly and didn't want anything to do with me, then who would? I was embarrassed and ashamed. I wanted so badly to fit in with the pretty girls and to be seen as pretty by the boys at school. But that never happened. I ended up getting over this incident (or so I thought), only to realize years later that it had a significant impact on how I allowed myself to be treated by the opposite sex. I learned that sometimes you sabotage your self-love subconsciously. Sometimes you are so hurt and broken deep down that you mistakenly believe that hurt has disappeared, when in actuality, it never left. It only manifested itself in other ways.

My freshman year of high school was a time I now look back on as an example of how my lack of self-love manifested itself in my relationships. I was excited about this next chapter of my life because as far as I was concerned, entering high school meant I was officially grown. As the youngest of five girls, I avoided the fate that all four of my sisters endured, being sent away to a private, all-girls, Catholic boarding school in Connecticut. I was the rebel who was adamant about staying home and attending public high school like the rest of my middle school friends. I was sure my parents were making a mistake in trying to send me away, and I just kept telling them there was no way I was moving to Connecticut. Luckily for me, Julian had some issues while she was at the school, which worked out in my favor. My parents allowed me to stay home and attend public school.

As I started high school, I still had issues with my lack of self-confidence and self-love (actually, I didn't even know what that was at the time). It wasn't as bad as earlier years, but it was still there. My insecurity reared its head when I noticed that most of my really pretty girlfriends had equally handsome boyfriends, or at least, boys chasing after them. Of course there was more to school than boys (I was on the honor roll throughout high school, thank you very much). But truth be told, I was seeking that same attention and put a lot of time and effort into my clothes, hair, and make-up (which consisted of eyeliner) every day. I didn't realize until later how much I thrived off compliments, especially when they came from guys.

Fall semester of my freshman year was my very first homecoming. A couple of months prior to that, I started dating a guy, who I'll call Tony. Tony was an upperclassman and had flirted with me for a little while before asking me to be his girlfriend. So I said "yes," not because I really liked him and was attracted to him, but because it made me feel worthy (and deep down, I didn't know when anyone else would ask). I felt pretty enough because someone had asked me to be his girlfriend. He was a boost to my self-confidence because he always told me how pretty I was. Having a boyfriend meant that I wouldn't have to attend homecoming without a date, although that's the story I told my parents. (Sorry Mom and Dad.) I had it all worked out; since we had a family gathering to attend later that evening, I arranged for my sisters to pick me up from the dance.

Tony and I met up at the homecoming dance, where we hung out with my girlfriends and their dates. We danced a little, and then about an hour later, he mentioned that he wasn't feeling well. He wanted to go home and change his clothes, and he asked me if I would go with him. He lived across the street from the school. Afraid that I would get the third degree from my friends, I didn't tell them I was leaving. I kind of just disappeared with Tony. Besides, I figured we'd only be gone for a few minutes.

It was the longest, most horrific few minutes of my life.

When we finally returned to school, everything was a blur. People were leaving, and my sisters and my friends had been looking for me. I barely remember saying two words before rushing into my sister's car and mumbling "bye" to my friends. All I wanted to do was go home, curl up, and disappear. Instead, I had to act as if everything was all right while we attended this family function.

I tried not to think about what had happened at Tony's house and acted as if nothing was wrong. I guess I must have put on an award-winning performance, because no one seemed to notice that deep down, I was in distress. I was hurting physically and emotionally. I remember going to use the bathroom while at this party. It was the first time I had used the bathroom since leaving homecoming and I wasn't prepared for what came next.

When I saw the amount of blood on my clothes, I was mortified. But at the same time, I had no one to turn to. I kept replaying the night in my head, like it was all a bad dream. I tried to retrace my steps to figure out how I could've been so naïve as to allow this to happen to me. Then I recalled a conversation I'd had with Tony several weeks before we became "official." He had asked me if I was a virgin, and when I told him I was, he wanted to know why. It was an awkward conversation because we never talked about sex in my household. Sex was a dirty word that only loose people used and engaged in. Then it clicked. Tony had asked me to be his girlfriend because he wanted one thing and one thing only: my innocence. But I didn't give it to him. He stole it. And I kept quiet about it because I thought it was my fault. Why else would a girl willingly leave a homecoming dance to go to her boyfriend's house if she wasn't asking for it? And who would believe her if she said otherwise?

See, I had no idea what love really was, let alone self-love. I felt ashamed, betrayed, and hurt. Needless to say, Tony broke it off with me shortly after he won his "prize." I had no choice but to continue acting as if nothing were wrong, since I still had to see him just about every day at school. The only person I ever confided in (until now) was my husband. He has been at the core of my healing.

The relationship with Tony led to many more bad ones before I started dating my husband four years later. I didn't realize how broken I was until I had someone that demonstrated true love, and loved me unconditionally—no strings attached, no expectations. For the first time, I was able to look in the mirror and truly love what I saw. And that was me.

If you're broken or feeling unloved, it's so important for you to take time out and pour love into yourself. I'm learning to pour love into my children every day because I don't ever want them to feel like they have to depend on the opposite sex to feel loved. I'm teaching them the importance of self-love now, while they're young. I want them to understand that they don't ever have to accept something that's not love, because there are a lot of counterfeits out there. Instilling confidence in my children is extremely important to me. Granted, I tell my kids they're beautiful all the time because they are. But when they turn around and tell me how pretty I am, and then exchange the same compliments with each other, it just makes my heart melt. We teach our children to respect, protect, and love one another at all times. I want to make sure that their "self-love muscles" get a good workout from early on.

Where was it in your life that you lost your self-love chain? Did you never receive it, or did it break off somewhere along the line?

FINDING YOUR SHOES

TWEET THIS! @WhoseShoesBook
There is no one that can love you better than you love yourself. #whoseshoes

Part of learning how to love yourself is learning how to let go of past hurts, grudges, and disappointments. Usually, the things we find hardest to let go of are the very things that are keeping us from reaching our next level of greatness.

1. Reflect.
Pull out your journal and start by answering these questions:

- How will you begin to feed love into your soul on a daily basis?

- What are some past hurts you need to let go of in order to move forward in this stage of your life?

- Who or what do you have to forgive (whether it's another person, yourself, or a situation) in order to truly love yourself?

- What lessons did you learn from these hurtful situations that have made you stronger and wiser?

- How will you use this newfound self-love to create change in the world?

While you may not be ready to do anything with this information right now, you will find it useful to write it down. As you reflect on your answers to these questions, you should notice a heightened awareness of things you may not have even known you were still holding on to. When you think about the things that tense you up or anger you, there's a good chance that's where you need to start letting go.

2. Affirm.

If you're not sure of where or how to start, then these affirmations will help you. Write them down, put them somewhere you can easily see them, and recite them on a daily basis. Words are powerful; the more you speak them out loud, the more you will see and feel a shift in how you feel about yourself.

- I am beautiful.

- I am smart.

- I am worthy.

- I forgive myself for _____.

- I love myself because _____.

- I give myself permission to be great.

- I believe in myself, even when those around me don't.

- I have a purpose that I will walk in.

- I am determined and will live to see my dreams manifest.

- I don't need validation from anyone else to be great.

- I don't need validation from anyone else to be successful.

- Success is what I want it to be and not what others want it to be for me.

- I am confident.

- I am sexy.

- I love myself.

5 WHO TOLD YOU YOU WERE JERRY MAGUIRE? YOU DON'T NEED ANYONE TO COMPLETE YOU
JULIAN

A house that is built by God will be completed. —Ethiopian Proverb

Most of us remember that scene in one of the most romantic movies of all time, where Tom Cruise, acting as Jerry Maguire, a successful sports agent, looks at the woman he's about to lose and utters the magic words that get him the girl: "You . . . complete me."

Wow! What woman wouldn't want to hear those words from the man she fantasized about spending the rest of her life with? If you're like me, you grew up reading romance novels and watching romantic movies that gave an utterly unrealistic picture of what love really is and what relationships are about. We are raised to practically worship the white dress and begin planning our wedding day the minute we're old enough to wear a training bra. We look forward to the day that we will finally be "complete" and married to the Prince Charming of our dreams, our Knight in Shining Armor, who will be the period at the end of our Cinderella story.

Except for some reason, all we keep attracting are tadpoles, frogs, and grasshoppers (the kind that hop from one woman to another).

And we just can't figure out why. I'm going to share a secret with you that took me a long time to finally figure out.

TWEET THIS! @WhoseShoesBook
When you look for others to complete you, you send a message that you're broken so you will keep attracting other broken people. #whoseshoes

You don't need another human being to complete you. The only person who can do that is your Creator. If you're not already complete when you embark on any relationship, all you're going to get is two broken people trying to give what they just don't have. The person that you spend the rest of your life with should enhance who you already are, *not* be responsible for completing you. That's your job. And it's not necessarily an easy one.

You cannot be complete and whole without first dealing with your wounds from the past and taking the time to heal them. I don't know anyone who isn't emotionally wounded in some way. If you're alive and breathing, then at some point in your life you have been hurt by someone you cared about.

People deal with pain in different ways. They either hold on to it like a badge of honor and force others to work overtime to prove how much they really care; or, they take it for what it is, deal with it, and then do what it takes to heal that wound so that it no longer has power over them. Forgiveness of yourself and others is a huge part of that equation. Without it, you will continue operating from a place of pain, and make other people responsible for healing that which only God can heal. I learned this lesson the hard way.

At twenty-three, I was living my life like it was golden. I had graduated from college magna cum laude, landed a well-paying job in my field, and was getting ready to marry the man of my dreams—or so I thought. I think there should be a law against getting married before you're thirty. Most of us have no idea who we are or what we really want from a life partner—or even from life—in our twenties. We're still figuring things out. But here I was, someone who had always known what I wanted, making a lifelong commitment that would prove to be life-changing.

When I met Michael (not his real name) through mutual friends, while still in college, I initially wasn't looking for a relationship. I didn't know what I wanted from a relationship, except for what I had read in romance novels. In fact, I didn't even consider him my type. You know: the Idris Elba type. Or Morris Chestnut. Or Boris Kodjoe. Or . . . well, you get the point.

What started out as a good friendship, turned into a full-blown relationship. In the course of dating for two years before getting married, I don't think we ever once talked about our expectations as husband and wife. Subconsciously, I was thinking, "Great! I get to check off one more thing on my to-do list and marry someone who is acceptable to my parents." Not only was Michael the same religion, he was from the same country and the same ethnic group, and was loved by my friends and family. He "completed me." And my mental checklist.

Michael did more for me than any other man had done in my past relationships (the bar, unfortunately, wasn't that high), so I took what he was willing to give, not knowing that I should have demanded more. A lot more. You see, growing up in a culture and a household where showing outward affection wasn't the norm, I never really saw my parents being affectionate toward one another or even towards us. That was what they knew. And I realize now that having been starved for that affection growing up, I looked for it in the opposite sex as a way of feeling "complete" and validated. It's something that is all too common for many of us.

So when Michael came along, and paid me all this attention—surprised me with trips to events that he knew I would enjoy and told me I was funny, beautiful, and sweet—I just knew I had hit the jackpot. When it was time for me to choose my life partner, he was the logical choice. Partly because ours was the longest relationship I had ever been in, and partly because I loved him in the way that I understood love to be defined back then. And did I mention that he met all the requirements to be acceptable to my parents?

I remember being caught up in planning the wedding, which was a major production. We were one of the first couples in our generation to get married in our community—a community which had seen me grow up from toddlerhood, to adulthood, and now, soon-to-be-wife. You know that old adage, "It takes a village to raise a child"? Well, let's just say that the entire "village" expected to attend the wedding. And with six hundred guests, you could say that close to the entire village did. What can I say? It was an African wedding.

But here was the thing: amidst all of the planning and excitement of being the center of attention, despite all of the support and love we received from the "village," there was something very wrong. Do you remember that still, small voice I talked about in Chapter Three? Well, I should have been paying closer attention to it throughout the entire relationship. There were signs I saw (little white lies, broken promises, and manipulation, and my discomfort about certain things Michael did), but I was so intent on portraying the right image and doing what was expected of me that I ignored them all. There were even times he would lie to someone right in front of me because he was trying to avoid unpleasantness or confrontation. If there's one thing I've learned, it's that if someone will lie to someone else in *front* of you, they will certainly lie *to* you.

On my wedding day, I woke up feeling . . . nothing. But I figured it just was fatigue from all the partying the night before. In our culture we have a pre-wedding party called a Kasiki, which is similar to an engagement party. Why we do it the night before the big day, I really don't know. Besides, I was drained from all the preparations and planning it had taken to get us to the actual day. I ignored the uneasy feeling in my stomach that morning and attributed it to just being a little "out of it." So out of it, that while sitting at the altar as the priest was speaking to us about the commitment we were about to make in front of all these witnesses, all I could think was, "I wonder what people would think if I just walked away from this altar and left the church. For good." But of course I couldn't do that. We had paid a lot of money for this wedding and had people fly in from all over the country and the world to join us in what was supposed to be a joyous occasion.

And so I went through the day in a haze, with my "Happy Mask" fully intact. It was like I was an actress watching this incredibly joyful event unfold right before my eyes while I willed myself to be truly happy and 100% present in the moment. Instead, I was trying to fight an apathy that I couldn't understand. I mean, I was marrying the man who completed me and validated me as a person. What woman wouldn't be happy about that?

Throughout the five years we were married, there were some great times and not-so-great times. During those years, I kept a journal. When I went back and read my entries after our divorce, they were very telling as to my frame of mind while I was with Michael. In looking for someone else to complete me, I found myself unknowingly still restless and emotionally disconnected within my marriage. I recognized, after the fact, that because I was so broken inside and in need of my own healing, I had attracted someone with similar issues, who couldn't give me what I needed because he didn't have it to give. But that didn't excuse his behavior. All of the things that I should have paid more attention to before I said "I do" became magnified.

At the point when I knew something was wrong but couldn't put my finger on exactly what was happening to us, I confronted Michael and asked him if he was having an affair. Why else would he go out of town "for work" so much more often than he used to, get a second cell phone, and be so distant? He denied it, and I accepted his denial, because it was what I wanted to hear. But even then, I knew. Deep down, I knew that this man, who I had vowed to love for better or for worse, was lying to me. I didn't want to believe it because it would ruin my Cinderella fairy tale.

When I found out I was pregnant in our fifth year of marriage, things were still shaky between us, but I hoped that the baby would plug whatever holes were causing our boat to slowly sink. *Then* we would be complete. And live happily ever after. Not.

TWEET THIS! *@WhoseShoesBook*
You can't fix a ship that's already halfway underwater.
#whoseshoes

Things went downhill quickly after my daughter was born. Michael grew even more distant, became argumentative, spent less time at home, and seemingly turned into someone I didn't recognize as the person I had married. I say "seemingly" because the negative characteristics he exhibited during that time were things that I had already known about him but chose to ignore. Our rocky ending only magnified them. After much prayer, counseling and, what seemed like unending tears, God made it clear to me that if I didn't get myself and my daughter (who was nine months old at that time) out of that environment, I could easily spiral into a deep depression. It finally got to a point where I realized that the very thing I had thought was going to complete me was actually poisoning my spirit.

Although I gave my marriage everything I had and did the best I could with what I knew then, it wasn't enough. Despite confirmation from close friends that Michael had been having an affair—probably throughout the majority of our marriage—I eventually realized, even without that devastating discovery, our marriage would still have failed for many reasons. Not the least of which was the fact that, deep down, I had known even before we started planning the wedding that I was with him more for convenience, comfort, and the idea of completion, than I was because I could genuinely see myself happily spending the rest of my life with him. But it took me a long time, a lot of work, and the willingness to forgive him and myself to admit that uncomfortable truth.

"And in all things, God works for the good of those who love Him and are called to His purpose." (Romans 8:28). This was certainly the case with my broken marriage. Not only did I give birth to a beautiful daughter, I received the greatest gift of all: freedom and space to heal and to discover who I really was, what I really wanted, and what God put me here to do. Don't get me wrong; the months following my divorce were the most excruciating I had ever been through—especially when I found out that Michael fathered a child by another woman less than five months after our separation. Unless you've been through it, it's not something you can really understand. That experience made me realize that a marriage is truly a living, breathing thing, and that when it ends, it's like the death of someone you love. The grief was just unbearable at times.

There were moments when I felt like I was in a perpetual black hole, a nightmare that I didn't deserve to be living in. Many times, I would go driving aimlessly just to be alone and scream and cry and ask why. Why me? Why us? Why now? This wasn't how I had planned my life. This wasn't part of the script. There were even times when—if it meant the pain would go away—I would consider a reconciliation with Michael. But when I thought about the reasons why, they had less to do with love and everything to do with convenience (I knew him), comfort (he was predictable), and completion (we were *supposed* to be a family). Those were the reasons that had landed me here in the first place. It was time to move on and allow myself time to be open to whatever God had next for me.

Throughout the process of grieving, I prayed for three things:

• That my pain wouldn't be wasted and God would allow me to use that experience and everything I learned from it to help others through their own difficult times;

• That I wouldn't become bitter, but instead become better;

• That I would be restored a hundred-fold and live life more fully than I had before my divorce.

God has been faithful to my prayers. In the ten years since my marriage ended, I have had amazing opportunities come my way, traveled the world, reached just about all of my goals, and checked quite a few items off my bucket list. Going through that experience played a big part in my healing and becoming content and complete as my own person. The most important part of becoming complete was learning that real love wasn't that fleeting nonsense that only happens in fairy tales and romance novels. Real love starts with learning who you are as a child of God and learning to love yourself with all your faults and in all of your imperfect fabulosity so that you can attract that same love into your life.

Because I took the time to do my work and take accountability in the part I played in allowing certain people and circumstances into my life that caused me pain, I have been able to use the pain to push me out of my comfort zone and into my purpose. It's an ongoing process—all growth is—but the rewards of going through it far outweigh the benefits of staying stuck in "incomplete" mode for the rest of your life.

So how do you go about becoming complete as your own person instead of waiting on others to validate you? After getting through my divorce, this was the hardest work I have ever done. As with all things that force you to grow, it takes commitment, a level of self-awareness you may not be used to, and unrelenting focus on becoming the person you were intended to be. But you have to first be clear on what that is. And here's the wonderful thing about this process:

TWEET THIS! @WhoseShoesBook
Everything you are destined to be is already inside you, so there's nothing you have to make up.
#whoseshoes

Your job is to peel away the layers (you might need a jackhammer for a few of them) that are hiding the real you.

First things first. You need to ask yourself, where in the world did you ever get the idea that you were incomplete? You may never have had that conscious thought, but if you are always looking outward for validation, then this is you. Read the following questions and if you answer "yes" to any of them, then we've got work to do.

1. Do you find it difficult to make a decision without first consulting every single person in your phone book? (Okay, that's a bit of an exaggeration for some, but if you find yourself indecisive about a number of things in your life, then your answer would be "yes.")

2. Are you someone who finds yourself only happy when you are the center of attention—all the time?

3. Are you all about the "bling" and making sure that everyone notices you with it—whether it's a car, nice jewelry, expensive shoes, or designer clothing? (Note that there's a difference between buying things because you enjoy the benefits they afford and appreciate the quality, and buying expensive stuff to mask your own

insecurities. Only you can tell the difference. Be honest.)

4. Do you find it difficult to be in your own company and actually enjoy it for even short periods of time?

5. Are you a relationship addict and unable to remain single because, to you, that means you're not desirable?

6. If you were to define who you are, does that definition only depend on your relationship to other people? (e.g., wife, mother, daughter, friend, sister, aunt, etc.)

7. Do you get easily discouraged for prolonged periods of time when your contributions are not recognized by people who you feel matter?

8. Do you find yourself in unhealthy relationships where you feel disrespected, unappreciated, belittled, or even abused because you're more concerned about another person's feelings than you are about your own self-worth?

9. Is it customary for you to make other people prove how much they care about you by constantly stroking your thirsty ego?

Whew! We've got issues, don't we? First, take some comfort in that. Not in the fact that you have issues, but that you can recognize you're not the only one struggling with these challenges. And then pat yourself on the back, because you had the wisdom and the will to buy this book (thank you!), which means that you are ready to do something life-changing to become the person you really want to be. So grab your journal and pen, and let's get to writing!

Keep in mind that in order for this to work—for true

transformation to take place—you're going to have to be brutally honest with yourself. You're going to have to keep it *real*. We're going to ask you throughout this book to get really uncomfortable with your feelings and dig deep so we can get to the heart of why you do what you do. As you go through what may be a painful process, remember these words I first heard from Iyanla Vanzant:

TWEET THIS! @WhoseShoesBook
You can't heal what you won't reveal. #whoseshoes

Even the Bible says that the truth will set you free. (John 8:32) Once you deal with certain truths, they no longer have power over you.

FINDING YOUR SHOES

1. Identify your vices.
Think back to the very first time you can remember seeking someone's validation and approval and then answer the following:

- Who was that person (or people)? Did they give you the approval you sought?

- Did they only approve of you when you did what they expected of you, or did they provide you with unconditional love?

- Have you always felt like you were incomplete and needed something to fill that void?

- What vices have you used to fill that void?

- How did it make you feel every time you realized that that feeling of being complete and happy was only temporary when you looked for something or someone else to complete you?

- How do you think this has affected your relationships with others?

- Why do you think you are *not* complete as you are now?

- What does being complete look and feel like to you?

- Is there anyone in your life who you think embodies the idea of being complete? If so, what are three characteristics that you admire about them?

- What role does God play in filling the void you have inside of you?

Take your time answering these questions. It may be the first time you've had to really think about what it means to self-validate. This is one of those things that takes a gradual mind-shift. No one wakes up one day and automatically sheds bad habits, relationships, and behaviors. Change happens one day, one answer, one decision at a time. Even after doing my own work, I still find I have to remind myself not to return to certain habits that I had given up. Don't worry if you find that you have a hard time making this shift. I can't stress this enough: it takes time. Be patient with yourself. Keep in mind that whatever age you are is how long it's taken you to develop the habits and ways of thinking that have gotten you to where you are now. It's going to take time, and a whole lot of patience and persistence to change that.

Think of it as if you were a house that was built years ago. Over the years, every tenant comes and paints each room a different color, installs different flooring, and makes various additions to parts of the home. Each tenant leaves their own indelible mark on the property.

Each adds a layer of their own preference. When a new tenant comes in and decides that they want to now completely renovate the entire home, they have to first: do a thorough inspection, including making sure that the house has a sound foundation; taking notes on what changes need to be made; determining what new materials they want to use; developing new design plans; and hiring a brilliant team to bring that vision to life.

The team has to go in and remove everything that no longer works. That means securing the foundation if it's shaky. That means peeling off all those layers of paint and wallpaper and flooring and getting rid of pests that may be hiding in the crevices. That includes buying new appliances, materials, doors, and windows and filling the house with beautiful color and quality furniture that will stand the test of time. Sometimes it requires a complete gut job. But it doesn't happen overnight. And if it's not done right from the bottom up, the foundation will begin to crack, and you'll have to do all those renovations all over again. Let's make sure to put your house in proper order now, so you don't have to go back and fix a cracked foundation or replace cheap furniture down the line.

Just like building a home, you have to begin with your end goal in mind—your vision for what you want to see at the end of your "renovation." The Bible says, "Write the vision and make it plain." (Habakkuk 2:2) And you have to be patient because there may be unexpected "expenses" or additional "renovations" that need to be completed upon further inspection, so you can stick a "Lifetime Warranty" sticker on that baby when all is said and done!

This next exercise will help you begin those renovations.

2. Get comfortable with you.

When was the last time you went somewhere by yourself and had a good time *by* yourself? This is your challenge. Find someplace where you can go—a park, a trip, a restaurant, a party, even—alone. Focus on just being in the present moment and enjoying your own company. Consider it your time to just do you. Don't worry about what you think everyone else may be thinking about you. Chances are, no one cares. Most of us are so caught up in our own lives that we don't have the time to worry about what anyone else is or isn't doing. Note: You are not allowed to use your cell phone as a crutch. You know how we do when we get uncomfortable being alone in public. We pull out that trusted phone like it's a lifeline! Understand that you can be alone without being lonely.

The most important thing is that you use this as an opportunity to get comfortable with being with you. Appreciate the fact that you can have a good time by yourself, and celebrate that accomplishment. Learn to do this often, and engage in other activities that allow you to venture out on your own. As you become comfortable with yourself, you will no longer depend on others to make you happy and will, instead, be well on your way to being complete in and of yourself. You'll also find that you open yourself up to the opportunity to interact with others from a place of vulnerability (not a bad word) and authenticity.

3. Pray, meditate, and ask.
Find time to regularly pray and meditate, asking God to show you how to uncover and address those things that keep you stuck looking for other things to fill what only He can. I usually keep a journal close by whenever I do this because the wisdom that comes out of these sessions is invaluable. Don't give up if you don't hear anything right away or if you find yourself unable to focus. Practice makes perfect. If you're not used to being still and listening, then this is one more habit you'll have to cultivate in order to become more in tune with your inner voice. Keep at it, and make it a regular habit. It will help you keep your pipeline to hearing His voice clear. I make it a point to

spend the first thirty minutes before I get out of bed in the mornings, and at least the last fifteen minutes before I end my day, all about my dialogue with God. It helps me stay centered.

As you go through this phase of learning how to just do you, ask God to fill you with the grace and wisdom that can only come with regular time in His presence. The more time you spend with Him, the more you'll realize that, to get all you really want, you have to understand that He is all you really need.

6 "NO" IS A COMPLETE SENTENCE
CHRISTINE

Setting personal boundaries is about protecting and caring for yourself. It's about learning how to say "no" to others, so you can say "yes" to you.
—*Christine K. St. Vil*

"No" is one of the first words we comprehend when we learn how to talk. I remember all three of my children going through the "no" phase. Everything was "no," even when they really meant "yes." But as adults, how many times do we say "yes," when we really want to yell "no"? How do we go from saying it so freely as babies, to being so scared to say it as adults? Why is it so difficult for us to just say no?

From my own experience, I now know that my inability to say no and turn people down was due, in large part, to my insecurities and lack of self-esteem. We didn't grow up in a household where we were allowed to test the waters or challenge people (especially our elders) by saying no. If we were asked to do something or go somewhere, it went without saying that we had to do it—no questions asked. On the flip side, the word "no" was a regular part of my parents' vocabulary. I remember dreading it any time I had to ask my parents' permission to do anything fun because I knew that nine times out of ten, the answer would be "no." So I would usually wait until my Dad wasn't around, and ask my mom (she was the more lenient of the two), only for her to say, "You'll have to ask your Dad when he gets home." And you know what he said when I asked, right? "No."

"No" to going trick-or-treating (a couple of times they got really tired of our whining and allowed it); "no" to hanging out with friends after school; "no" to sleepovers; "no" to piercing my ears (which didn't happen until one of my best friends surprised me and took me on my 18th birthday). The word "no" had such a negative connotation for me growing up, that looking back, I can see its direct effect on my perception of rejection into adulthood. That feeling of rejection is something I struggled with for a while.

I now understand that I equated the word "no" to rejection. Because we were never given a reason as to why we couldn't do certain things, I never really understood how to deal with rejection. As I got older, I took it personally. If I wanted something or asked for something and was refused, I took it as an attack. If I applied for a position and didn't get it, I was really hurt. I couldn't see past the rejection to the fact that there was probably something for me to learn from it. All I could see was that I had failed in some way. It took me back to my childhood rejection every time. Was I not good enough? Was I not pretty enough? Was I not talented enough?

In high school when the very first step team was being formed, I was excited. Finally, something I could do, especially after making a fool out of myself by trying out for the basketball team. (I figured my height would give me an advantage. Not.) For once in my adolescent years, I was confident. While there was a lot of competition at tryouts, I just knew I had this. I had every move down pat, and I was one of the strongest steppers trying out. As a matter of fact, I was so good, I thought I deserved to lead the team. So you can imagine my shock when I went to check the list of people who had made the team, and my name wasn't on the list.

Instead, there were several people on the list that had screwed up at tryouts and had about as much rhythm as Carlton Banks doing his signature dance on *The Fresh Prince*. But they were more popular. They were prettier. They wore the latest designer clothes and shoes. It became clear that it had become a popularity tryout. That "no" was a slap in the face because it made me realize that it didn't matter how good I was; I didn't fit in, so I wasn't needed. It was a horrible feeling for me in that moment—to be told no when I really wanted and deserved to hear a "yes."

When you think about your inability to say no to certain people or requests, where does that stem from for you? What was true for me was the notion of not wanting to hurt people's feelings. I felt that if someone was asking me for something and I had the ability to help, then why would I refuse? Why would I subject them to the same rejection that I experienced if it was in my power to say yes?

I liked being depended upon when someone needed something. It gave me a sense of validation. In some ways, I felt like it made me thrive. I thought it made me a better person to always be available for everyone else. But more often than not, it stressed me out, leaving me exhausted and overwhelmed, which eventually caused me to function ineffectively as a mother and a wife. What is it costing you to not set boundaries?

Some time back I posted the following on my Facebook fan page:

"At a women's conference I attended in 2012, Lisa Nichols said something that made a major impact on me. She said that we need to learn how to give only when our cup is overflowing. How many times do we give and give only to feel more empty and less fulfilled? It's because we repeatedly empty our own cup, instead of waiting for it to spill over and serving only from the overflow. Sometimes we have to be what some might view as selfish in order to maintain our self-care. How can you commit to giving only from your overflow?"

This was one of the responses that I received:

"But my cup has never overflowed, and that can be very subjective, but does that truly mean I have nothing to give?"

My answer to this question is this: It may not necessarily mean you have nothing left to give. But, what is it costing you? What are the sacrifices you are making in order to give what you barely have for yourself? For me it was costing me my health. Mentally and physically, I was exhausted and overwhelmed. I was taking out my frustration from overloading my own plate on my husband and kids. They were the ones who had to deal with my poor attitude and lack of energy.

You know that term, "Don't bite off more than you can chew"? It applies when figuring out how to set boundaries for yourself. When you start to feel like your head is spinning, and you're about to curl up into the fetal position, or you just don't know how you're going to get through another one of those days, it's time to stop. Stop and reevaluate just how much food you've piled onto your plate. Is there any room for the main course (you), or have you packed it all up with side dishes (everyone and everything else)?

When you look back at your childhood, what are some of the mannerisms you see in yourself, which your parents (or guardians) displayed? For example, my father always had a very short temper, and was quick to yell first and ask questions later. Just as my father has gone through his own transformation in that respect (we can't believe the stuff he let's his grandchildren get away with), I also have had to go through mine. I used to be just as short-tempered and quick to yell. Although I've come a long way, God definitely isn't through with me yet.

I've learned that I have to catch myself with my own children because I don't want to do the same thing in making them feel attacked anytime they want to talk. I want them to feel comfortable talking to me about anything, whether it's good or bad. I know that if

I react in the same manner that my father did with us, I might close off that important gateway to communication. Although my children hear no from me (let's not get it twisted, they can't get whatever they want all the time), I still make a conscious effort to understand what it is they are asking, and why I am saying no. An important lesson learned from my own experience.

God knew what he was doing when he blessed me with my husband. Lord knows that if he hadn't been equipped with as much patience as he has, we probably wouldn't have made it through to eight years of marriage. One of the things I've always loved about Phillip is the fact that he doesn't get bent out of shape at the drop of a dime. He's usually the one to calm me down when I get a little heated, so it's a blessing in more ways than one. He almost always knows when I need a break, and he never hesitates to make sure that I get it. Sometimes a simple trip to Panera is all I need to refill my cup (literally and figuratively). When you take time to pour love into yourself, everyone benefits from it.

I've learned the importance of setting boundaries for myself by learning how to say no. Yes, sometimes even to my own mama! I call it the three Rs: recharge, reconnect, and rediscover. You can learn how to take time out for yourself by treating yourself without spending a lot of money. However, it comes at a cost: the price of learning how to say no and setting boundaries to protect your space. No time? Create it. No support? Find it. Make the choice to make *you* a priority by adding you to your calendar. If you need to, take initiative and create your own community of support.

TWEET THIS! @WhoseShoesBook
We can do it all; we just can't do it all alone.
#whoseshoes

There are plenty of people out there who are ready to support you, but you have to be the one to reach out and ask for the help.

When we have an important client to meet with, or an important staff meeting or doctor's appointment scheduled, we do everything in our power to make sure we don't miss it, because we know we can't afford to. We need to treat ourselves just like that "can't miss" appointment, because we can't afford not to. If going for a walk by yourself is what would make you happy, then put it on your calendar, and don't stand the boss up. (Ahem . . . that would be you!)

Set boundaries. It's easier said than done, but it's doable. Decide now what you will commit yourself to when it comes to your family and friends. I come from a large family (I'm one of seven and have nine nieces and nephews—as well as my own three little ones), and have been blessed with an abundance of dynamic friends in my life. The problem? There is always something going on. Always. If it's not a birthday party, it's a baby shower. If it's not a baby shower, it's a wedding, a graduation, or just a plain ol' gathering of some sort.

I used to feel obligated to attend every blessed event that someone in my family or any of my close friends hosted, but when you start having kids of your own, things can get a little tricky. It takes longer to get out the door. It takes a lot more energy to entertain children while you're at a function, often times to the point where you can't even pay attention to whatever it is you're attending. And when you have to drive an hour one way to get to where you need to be, it's draining, especially for people like me who really don't like driving.

So although I don't love my friends or family any less, I do love myself a lot more these days. I love myself enough to know when I need a break. I love myself enough to know when I'm too tired to get my three young kids out the door. And I love myself enough to understand that I have my own family now, and they are my priority. Once I realized all of this, I felt a newfound sense of freedom, and a weight was lifted off my shoulders.

While I strive to make as many family functions as possible, and to be there for my friends when I can, I no longer break my neck to attend everything (although to some people it may look like I do). Instead, I set boundaries for myself so that I can serve from my overflow. One way I did this was to schedule a "Do Nothing Weekend" (DNW) once a month. This meant that if someone invited us to an event and it fell on my DNW, then they got a TBNT (thanks, but no thanks).

To figure out what you should start saying "no" to, take five minutes today to write out your priorities when it comes to your family, friends, and community. Are there some things that you can let go of or do less frequently? Can you limit the number of events you attend monthly? If you're constantly feeling like you have too much to do, and not enough time, it's probably because you haven't mastered the use of the word "no" yet. As my business coach always says, "We are always in choice!" When I am feeling overwhelmed and stressed, I now have to take a step back and realize that I'm the only one who can add or remove things from my plate.

And yes, there are times where emergencies may arise. However, let's be sure not to confuse someone else's emergency with our own. When you've spent years being there for everyone else, even if it meant not being there for yourself, it takes time to get used to saying no. I like to be dependable and reliable for those that matter to me, but I also had to start evaluating whether or not I was elevating their needs above my own. I recently read a quote that said, "When you say 'yes' to others, make sure you're not saying 'no' to yourself." No. One of the shortest words, but also one of the most powerful. It gives us a sense of confidence and rediscovery.

Caring for yourself is essential and should be non-negotiable. It's an act of survival. But you don't want to just survive; you should be aiming to thrive.

FINDING YOUR SHOES

How do you take your power back by learning to say no?

1. Identify.

What do you need to say no to? Realize that it may not be a permanent no, but a "no for now." Understand that you have to say no when:

- You are stressed and overwhelmed;
- You are exhausted or under the weather;
- Your plate is already overcrowded.

2. Decide.

Often, when we don't say no, we get caught up in other people's drama. Then we become resentful because we didn't set those boundaries for ourselves. Remember to say no when it's not your emergency to deal with, especially when:

- It's not something you want to do;
- It prevents you from doing something you really want to do;
- You feel your boundaries have been crossed;
- It takes you away from your true priorities.

3. Reflect.

What in your life do you need to say no to?

What stops you from saying no?

What are your beliefs about people who say no?

How do you feel when you say yes to something you really want to say no to?

TIP: If you have a hard time saying no, try starting with, "Let me think about it and get back to you," and then get back to them and say no.

Be sure to sign-up at www.whoseshoesbook.com for the complete worksheet and action steps to learn about the power of saying no.

7 GETTING RID OF EXCESS BAGGAGE: THE ULTIMATE WEIGHT LOSS SOLUTION
JULIAN

A man of many companions may come to ruin, but there is a friend who sticks closer than a brother. —*Proverbs 18:24*

A few months ago, I had an epiphany: The "seven-year-itch" is real. About every seven years, I get the itch to shed my old skin and reveal a newer, shinier, clearer one. In the last chapter of my book of life, my character was a people-pleaser and yes-woman, doing things just because other people thought I should. When it dawned on me that I had unintentionally given away my power by allowing people in my space who had either lost the right to be there or had never earned it to begin with, it forced me to rethink some of my decisions, especially when it came to my circle of online and offline friends.

Have you ever looked at yourself in a situation and realized that you really didn't want to be there? But because a good "friend" of yours had guilted you into doing what they wanted you to do, there you were, miserable and feeling manipulated and used, but not knowing how to say no to your friend. I'm here to tell you, a real friend doesn't manipulate—period. A real friend is someone who's got your back no matter what, takes the time to ask you how you're doing and actually listens when you respond, knows how to bring a smile to your face even when you have poison darts coming out of your eyes, and can speak truth to you without being spiteful or hurtful. A real friend sticks around, especially when the going gets tough, and gives you their shoulder to lean on, cry on, and rest upon. (Just don't wear out your welcome.)

As I took inventory of my various circles of "friends," I recognized that if I were to ever reach my potential and fulfill my dreams, I had to cut the dead weight and be deliberate about who I allowed in my circle. Over the years, I have had friends come and go. With some of them, we just lost touch and went our separate ways, while with others, the umbilical cord was severed very intentionally.

One particular situation I remember vividly involved a woman— I'll call her Joan—I met several years ago. We both attended one of the many events that go on in DC on any given day and bumped into each other afterwards. In our first encounter, I remember being impressed with the self-assured way she carried herself, how magnetic her personality was, and how warm and friendly she seemed—not to mention gorgeous. Her job was high-profile, her phone book was impressive, and her confidence was through the roof, or so I thought. And you would have too, if you saw the way that she worked a room regardless of who was in it. She seemed to always know how to make others feel as if they were long-lost friends and were the complete center of her attention.

In the course of a few weeks, Joan and I became fast friends and were almost inseparable. We must have talked five times a day and went everywhere together. She would share her boyfriend problems with me and I would share my lack of any with her (potential didn't count). We became so close, so quickly, that it was almost like an addiction. An unhealthy one. Before your imagination goes running wild, this wasn't exactly a fatal attraction type of friendship, but it was somewhat all-consuming. That should have been the first sign of something not being quite right. Note: If you ever come across anyone who, from your first meeting, seems too intense, they may have an addictive personality. Be on guard. More often than not, those types use that ability to create intensity in their relationships as a way to manipulate.

What I hadn't realized was that while I was busy singing her praises and saying nothing but great things about her, she was busy trampling my reputation—and our friendship—by talking negatively about me behind my back. Only it didn't stay behind my back for long. I found out very publicly what she really thought of me when I was accidentally copied on an e-mail that was sent out to a number of friends and colleagues we had in common. In the e-mail, she was berating me and belittling my ideas, and encouraging others to do the same. I was so shocked, I wasn't sure what to say. Talk about a curve ball.

See, the thing was, I have a strong personality myself and would like to think that I'm pretty charming (or so I've been told). I was just as capable of commanding attention when I needed to as Joan was. My sense of humor and ability to always see the good in people made it just as easy for me to make friends as it was for Joan. And in my mind, I thought we were going to be sistagirls for life because we were alike in so many ways and were intent on supporting one another in our goals. Um . . . nope.

I think in her mind, it was some kind of competition to see who could be the most popular, collect the most friends, and eventually garner the most recognition for her work. Sistas, this is why we haven't come as far as we should have by now and have such a hard time trusting one another. You do *not* need to compete with your fellow man (or woman).

As long as you always look at others as your competition, and not as potential allies, you will never be able to maintain genuine, meaningful friendships.

TWEET THIS! @WhoseShoesBook
The only person you should be competing with is
yourself. #whoseshoes

The sad thing is that, even after Joan's betrayal, I tried to talk
through the issue with her to find out why she had felt she had to go
that route instead of coming to me directly to discuss whatever issue
she may have had with me. I never really got a clear answer—lots of
excuses, including her sob story and profuse apologies, but no real
answer. For the sake of what I thought had been our friendship, I kept
trying to find a middle ground, where we weren't necessarily the best
of friends anymore, but at least we wouldn't be enemies. I was very
conscious of perpetuating the idea of Black women not getting along
and engaging in catty foolishness. Take Maya Angelou's advice on
this one: "The first time someone shows you who they are, believe
them." Value yourself enough to know when certain people no longer
deserve a place in your space. That is not to say that people don't
change, but it is to say that you don't need to be the collateral damage
for that change to happen.

It's taken me a while to learn this lesson, but I think I finally got
it: only surround yourself with people who you know have your back
no matter what, and who uplift, support, and add something positive
to your life. Life is too short to allow yourself to stay stuck with people
who leave you feeling emotionally exhausted and unsettled whenever
you're around them. If you are to ever accomplish what your heart
has laid out for you as your passion and purpose, you must have the
right people around you and get rid of those who no longer serve your
highest good.

In purging my own circle, I started with Facebook. Facebook,
although it has been a great tool for connecting and reconnecting

with friends, old and new, has also had its downside. Don't think that just because you're only friends with certain people in the virtual realm that their negative energy can't affect you in the physical.

Do you recognize any of these profiles in your own friendships (online or offline)?

- There's **"Negative Nancy,"** who can never seem to find anything good to say about anything and knows how to make, what should be a happy occasion, something to complain about. She posts every miserable thing that happens to her (including her stomach issues) online for you to see and sympathize with.

- Then there's **"Photo Opp Felicia,"** whose every post online is about how fabulous she is and what celebrity or politician she's met and managed to snag a picture with. Very few, if any, of her posts are about uplifting or supporting anyone else. It's all about shining the spotlight on herself. All the time.

- Let's not leave out **"Fairweather Fiona."** She's easy to find and connect with when all is going well in your life and it's all about the next party, but good luck trying to find her when things aren't going so great. Your calls go straight to voicemail, your messages go unanswered, and you're hard-pressed to find her when you need a shoulder to lean on.

- And we can't forget **"Gloomy Gabby,"** who is all about doom and gloom and will make sure you read every news article she can find about the sky falling, the economy failing, and the world ending. We know that there are problems in the world; we just don't need to be reminded of them. Every. Minute. Of the day.

- There's also **"Insecure Ingrid,"** who always makes you feel like you have to be careful of shining your own light too brightly around her, lest she get jealous or uncomfortable. You wouldn't want to offend her by allowing your brilliance to shine through, so instead you find yourself constantly dimming your light around her and being less of who God made you to be. My motto is:

 TWEET THIS! @WhoseShoesBook
You shouldn't dim your light to appease someone else's insecurities. If your light is too bright, let 'em get sunglasses. #whoseshoes

Then you have those friends you friended when you first joined Facebook, and although they're technically still your friends in the virtual world, they've outstayed their welcome in the real world. Yet, you feel guilty about removing them from your list because, well, they were your friend at one time. *Were* is the key word here. There's a quote by John F. Kennedy that speaks to this. "Change is the law of life. And those who look only to the past are certain to miss the future."

Letting go of certain relationships can be difficult, sometimes taking you on a guilt trip with all your luggage. But you have to ask yourself, what are you giving up or blocking out by holding on to something or someone whose chapter in your life already ended? Realizing that the life I envisioned was waiting for me on the other side of doubt and excess baggage, I sat down one weekend and purged my "friends" list on Facebook. In the process of going through my list and un-friending more than five hundred "friends" (yeah . . . it took a while), I realized that:

- I no longer wanted to do things out of obligation. Do you ever find yourself saying, "Well, we know so many people in common, and they made the effort to reach out. I really should accept their friend request." Don't do it. You should only connect with people because you want to, not because you feel obligated to.

- I'd outgrown many of those relationships. There were people who were part of my last chapter that just weren't meant to finish the rest of the book with me. As Ecclesiastes 3:1 says, "For everything there is a season . . . " Their season in my life was over.

- I only wanted to be surrounded by positive people. When you get to a certain place in your life and you're on fire with passion for your purpose, you find that you only want to be around people who are making a positive contribution to that energy. My rule of thumb is that if they leave you feeling down and depleted, then it's time to either cut them off or limit your interaction with them.

- I didn't want everyone in my business. I remember when I first joined Facebook, it was a popularity contest to see how many friends you could collect. But the older I get, the more I realize that it's more important to have a few really good friends, than it is to have hundreds of fair-weather ones.

- I wanted to make room for new relationships, blessings, and ideas to flow. If you keep holding on to things that God has told you to let go of, you're not leaving room for the amazing blessings that want to take their place. As one quote I recently read stated well:

TWEET THIS! @WhoseShoesBook
Cutting people out of my life does not mean
that I hate them. It simply means I respect me.
#whoseshoes

The process of un-friending people was surprisingly cleansing and especially empowering. It was like letting go of unnecessary baggage I didn't even know I was carrying. Talk about extreme weight loss. I should have done that sooner! If you're in a place in your life where you're reinventing yourself and reevaluating your relationships (which you probably are if you're reading this), this would be a great place to start. There's no time like the present to rethink the kind of energy you allow in your circle, as you boldly and fearlessly live out your purpose.

FINDING YOUR SHOES

1. Evaluate your circle.

Before you pull out the paper and pen, first think about your five closest friends, and then ask yourself:

- How do they make you feel when you are around them? Do you feel supported, safe, loved, positive, and/or powerful? *or* Do you leave interactions with them feeling emotionally drained and depleted?

- Are your friends goal-oriented and supportive of your goals?

- Is there always a sense of unspoken, unhealthy competition whenever you find yourself around them?

- Do you find yourself doing or saying things you regret later because of the influence of one or more of your friends?

- Have the people in your circle helped you to grow in a way that you can see the difference in who you are now versus who you were a year or two ago?

- Do you have a healthy spiritual connection with them that allows you to pray together, pray for one another, and/or share spiritual insights without feeling uncomfortable?

- Is your relationship a give-and-take? Do you each make mutual deposits into the friendship from which to make withdrawals?

- Has there been a betrayal of trust in your relationship that has never been acknowledged or healed?

- Do they validate how you feel, regardless of whether or not they agree with you?

TWEET THIS! @WhoseShoesBook
Forgiving someone doesn't mean you're obligated to give them back their place in your life. #whoseshoes

I think many times we make the mistake of saying, "Well, they apologized and seem really sorry for what they did, so I have an obligation to forgive and forget." Stop. Right. There.

Let me give you a visual. Say you were riding a bike and accidentally ran into a tree and broke your arm. Would you go back on that same bike (cast still on), intentionally run into that same tree, and ultimately break your other arm (or worse yet, the same arm in the same spot)? I would like to think that, although you might get back on that bike again, you would avoid that same tree which had already caused you so much pain. And so it is with friendships. Why would you go back to the same person that caused so much drama before? Note that the relationship with your spouse has a very different context than that with friends; therefore, these same principles may not necessarily apply.

Don't forget that you teach people how to treat you. Yes, the Bible says to forgive, but it also says that a companion of fools will suffer harm. (Proverbs 13:20) How many times will you need to learn the same lesson before you pass the test? If there's one thing I've come to understand, it's that the more quickly I learn what I need to learn from a particular situation or person and begin applying the lesson or principle, the sooner I can move on to the next chapter.

2. Be deliberate about your relationships.

Everyone in your inner circle should be adding something positive to it—whether it's unconditional love, much-needed laughter, sage advice, or unwavering support. If they're not adding something, it probably means they're taking something away. A good way to figure that out is to take a look at where you are in your life compared to your circle of friends. Actively seek out people who are more successful, smarter, and wiser than you, and who you can learn from. And remember that with any valuable relationship, it's a mutual give-and-take. Make sure you are also adding value to the relationship by being a useful resource and showing how you're putting any advice you receive into action.

Take the time to purge your "friends" list, both in the virtual and physical worlds. There are some people who may be offended, but there's nothing you can do about that. By keeping an eye on your vision for your life, you can determine if you see a particular person as part of your future. If not, then make peace with the fact that there may be people who don't understand, get upset, and want to berate you—but that's okay. It's not about them. It's about fulfilling your purpose with the right people by your side. That whole thing of birds of a feather flocking together is truth; if your closest friends are collectively not growing or doing anything positive with their lives, chances are, you aren't either.

Once you've purged, you want to then become very clear about the type of people you do want in your circle. Write a list of your values and the things that are non-negotiable in your relationships (e.g., mutual respect, support, positive outlook, etc.), and use that as a type of litmus test when it comes to anyone—male or female—with whom you may develop a relationship.

With family, it can get a little tricky because, as they say, you can pick your friends, but you can't pick your family. Even though you may not be able to completely avoid spending time around family members who are negative, you can certainly limit your time and interaction with them.

3. Become the friend that you want.

TWEET THIS! @WhoseShoesBook
You can't expect to get what you're not willing to give.
#whoseshoes

As you're going through your friends list, make sure to take some time to look in the mirror. Would you want to be your own best friend? If not, then doing the rest of the exercises in this book will not only get you to that point, you'll also begin attracting more like-minded people into your life.

Remember that as you go through this process, it may get uncomfortable or even painful, but know that the more focused you are on your vision for your life, the easier it will be to let go of the things, people, and situations that no longer serve you.

Note: A portion of this chapter appeared on www.boldandfearless.me.

8 TURNING OBSTACLES INTO OPPORTUNITY
CHRISTINE

You may encounter many defeats, but you must not be defeated. It may even be necessary to encounter some defeats to know who you are.

—Maya Angelou

Today, I am living the dream that I didn't even know I had. I am doing what I absolutely love. This year, I celebrated three years of freedom, and it feels so good! Three years ago (at the time of this writing), I became a stay-at-home-mom after walking away from my corporate job when I was six and a half months pregnant with my third child. It was the scariest thing I've ever had to do, but it has been the biggest blessing in my life. Because I was able to take that walk of faith, I've been able to pursue opportunities that I never even imagined. But it took going through a very low period to get to my high period. It took me losing myself as a woman and going through the darkness of postpartum depression in order for God to pull me through to see the light.

When I packed up my office and walked out of the corporate door in 2011, I felt this overwhelming sense of peace come over me. I didn't have an exit strategy or a plan because God had put me in a "holy discontent." My only focus was getting out of what was an unhealthy situation, in order to protect myself and the health of my unborn child.

It's funny how God works, because I'm not someone who had ever wanted or considered being a stay-at-home-mom. I always knew that I wanted to grow in my career and help other people along the way. Years ago, I had a conversation with God and told him what I wanted: to be married by twenty-five, have three kids, and be done with having kids by the time I was thirty-three. So far, God has answered my prayers. But I also had made plans to get back to work and continue to climb the corporate ladder. You know that saying, if you want to make God laugh, make plans? Well, God must have been having a good ol' laugh at my expense!

When I first left my job, I still had a few more months before the baby was due, so I decided to take on a consulting position for a recruiting firm. It was an opportunity for me to make a little more money, while having the added perk of working from home. I didn't really find the work to be exciting or fulfilling, and I couldn't figure out why because it was something I had been doing, and loving, for years. However, I continued to go through the motions because I wanted to make it work. I thought it was what God had planned for me, but I honestly never really took the time to ask. Or listen.

After I had my baby in June 2011, I continued to try to embrace my new role as a stay-at-home-mom. My kids loved having me home, and I enjoyed being home, but at some point, I began feeling restless. Going from a corporate working mom to a stay-at-home-mom overnight was a shock that I wasn't mentally prepared for. Even though I was happy that I wasn't dealing with the stress that I had been dealing with at work, I still wasn't being fulfilled. Deep down, I wasn't happy, but I couldn't express that, because from the outside looking in, I had no reason *not* to be happy. At a time when the economy was almost at it's worst, and people were struggling to find jobs, I was at a place where I didn't have to work outside of the home. I didn't have to worry about where money was going to come from or fear losing our home to foreclosure. I had three beautiful and healthy children, and the world's most amazing husband, who gave me everything I needed and anything I wanted.

Several months passed, and the feelings of unhappiness and discontent I thought I could just shake off were becoming more and more prevalent. It's such an ironic situation to be surrounded by so much love, and yet feel so isolated and unloved. I didn't love myself or anything about me. Somewhere along the way, I began to disengage from my children. I can't remember much of the first six to eight months of my daughter's life, because it was such a mental struggle. I was exhausted from the very beginning and don't think I ever got a chance to recuperate. Life for me as a stay-at-home-mom just kept moving full speed ahead, and I was desperately trying to keep up.

Two days after returning home from the hospital after giving birth to Brielle, my youngest, she had to be readmitted. Her jaundice, which she had been born with, had gotten worse. The medical condition, which all three of my children had causes yellowing of the skin or whites of the eyes due to an excess of the pigment, bilirubin. It is usually caused by the excessive breakdown of red blood cells or obstruction of the bile duct.

What we thought would be a few hours turned into almost five days. Five days away from home. Five days away from my other two children. Five days away from my husband. Five days of having to watch them prick my baby's foot to draw and then test her blood. Five days of barely any sleep because she had to be kept under the phototherapy lights most of the time, which meant I couldn't hold her as much. Five days of trying to consistently pump in order to keep my milk supply up, while supplementing with baby formula. It was exhausting, but we made it through and were so happy to get back home—at least for a little while.

Then when Brielle was twenty-eight days old (I will never forget the number of days because had she been a full thirty days, we wouldn't have had to go through this ordeal), she came down with a fever from a virus she contracted from her father. Because she was still less than a month old, she had to be admitted to Children's Hospital for them to diagnose the cause of the fever. I had to watch them stick her with several needles, and conduct multiple spinal taps. It turned out that she had a blood disorder called hereditary elliptocytosis, in which the red blood cells are abnormally shaped (much different from and milder than sickle cell), hence the battle with her stubborn jaundice. Again, what I thought would be a simple monitoring for a few hours, turned into needing two blood transfusions over the course of a few days, and spending another long week in a hospital.

Multiple hospital visits, lack of sleep, and the adjustment to being a stay-at-home-mom for the first time contributed to my extreme exhaustion and growing frustration. I literally cried from being so tired, and I had to call in the troops (my sisters) to come take turns to helping in the hospital. To this day, even with all that I have going on, I've never been more exhausted than I was during that time. After several months of feeling this way, I finally realized that something was very wrong. It took me a long time to understand that the thoughts and feelings I was having were not normal.

I remember several instances when Brielle cried; I just put her in her bassinet or crib, and looked at her, or walked away completely. I had no emotion. I just didn't care. I thought that I should be more engaged; I should *want* to pick her up. But I didn't. All I wanted to do was sleep. Even if my husband made time for me to nap before he went in to work at night, it was never enough. I don't feel like I would have ever harmed my children, but I knew that there was something wrong with my mental state. I didn't recognize it at the time, but I was suffering from postpartum depression (PPD).

In wanting to help other women who may be suffering through it,

I decided to do a feature article on Black And Married with Kids
(www.blackandmarriedwithkids.com—if you don't know about them,
check them out immediately!) with a doctor who treated women for
PPD to discuss how it affects women in the Black community.

TWEET THIS! @WhoseShoesBook
It is estimated that 1 in 5 women in the U.S.
experience Postpartum Depression. #PPD
#whoseshoes

Here's an excerpt from the interview I did on BMWK:

*"The hard part is [that] there is a gray line between postpartum blues
(which is more common), and postpartum depression (which is much
more serious). It can be hard to tell the difference, and some people
prefer not to expose that part of themselves. They don't want to seem
like they can't handle it.*

*What is the difference between postpartum blues (PPB) and PPD?
I think the biggest thing is the transient nature of the baby blues.
Mothers have moments or days in which they feel down, unworthy,
or just overwhelmed. That's a very common thing in the early parts of
the postpartum period. But it's interspersed with other parts of it that
they enjoy. They still enjoy their baby and still get pleasure out of their
child. There are up periods and not just downs. The ups will become
more frequent over time.*

*Depression tends to be much deeper and lasts much longer.
They don't get pleasure in dealing with the baby, and sometimes they
either feel negative or violent. It's hard sometimes for people to admit
it because it seems like such a 'bad mother' thing to feel negative
towards your baby. PPD is also much more dangerous [to yourself and*

your baby]. Unlike the baby blues, PPD will usually take some type of intervention (not necessarily medication)."

When I heard people talking about postpartum depression and the baby blues, I brushed it off because I felt like it was something other women went through. Not me. I had always looked forward to being a mother, and with a loving and supportive husband, I had everything I needed. But by the time our third child was born, I started to realize that no one was exempt from baby blues or PPD—not even myself. I didn't realize that my daughter's two hospital stays within her first month of life would have as great an impact on my mental health as they did.

It was months before I admitted, even to my husband, that things weren't quite right. I now know that I was a lot like other moms: embarrassed about feeling hopeless, overly exhausted, and disinterested in anything to do with motherhood. I'm so thankful that my case didn't take a severe turn for the worse. I know that there are women who do struggle with severe cases of PPD. I share this because I feel it is so important for women to understand that you are not alone. You are not a bad person because you don't have feelings for your child or you are having thoughts about hurting your child. You just need support, and you need help. So please don't feel ashamed in asking for it.

One resource which has a wealth of great information is Postpartum Progress (www.postpartumprogress.com). I don't think there is any question that hasn't been asked or addressed on the site as it relates to PPD. If you ever feel like you may be experiencing Baby Blues or PPD, then I encourage you to speak to your doctor immediately. The sooner you can address the problem, the better. I didn't address it because I hadn't recognized it as a problem. But I found that talking through it regularly with my husband, and making sure that I got regular mommy breaks to recharge, allowed me to get through it.

The real turning point in my life came when I began to look in the mirror, and not recognize the person I was becoming. I had gone from having pride in what I wore every day and how I styled my hair and makeup, to wearing no makeup, donning baggy clothes, and still looking like I was six months pregnant at nine months postpartum. Yup, I was a frumpy mom. I had completely let myself go.

I finally realized that I needed to get back to first loving myself. After some serious soul-searching, personal coaching, and a concentrated effort, I was able to make changes that helped me feel good on the outside, which in turn led to feeling great on the inside. I shed nearly thirty pounds of my baby weight that year—no secrets or anything fancy, just cutting out sweets and junk food—putting myself first in my list of priorities, and taking the time to pour love back into myself. It gave me confidence to do things that I normally wouldn't have done, to take some major steps out of my comfort zone. I knew God had released me from the corporate grind, and that He had allowed me to go through my period of PPD because there was a purpose to all of that. I just didn't know what it was at the time.

So I set out to find that purpose. I started networking and attending events that focused on women's empowerment and entrepreneurship. By this point, I knew that going back to work for someone else was not on the agenda on my journey to pursuing my purpose. People say to follow your passion, but when you're not quite sure what it is, it can get a little confusing and even frustrating. But I knew I had one. I just needed to get around the right people. I knew I had to start believing in myself and that I had to get over myself, to get over my fears that were keeping me from finding my purpose.

Shortly after I began this journey, I received an e-mail inviting me to an event for women discussing the ups and downs of entrepreneurship and what women needed to know to thrive. At this event, I met one of the co-authors of the book that was being featured. She invited everyone to her annual conference that was just a few weeks away. Not only did her powerhouse lineup of speakers intrigue me (Lisa Nichols, Suze Orman, and Jillian Michaels, to name a few), but the title of the conference and what she promised to deliver excited me: The Get RADICAL Women's Conference. I knew for sure that I needed a radical change in my life. I'd taken the first step in finding myself; now, I needed to take the next step in finding my purpose.

When I tell you that my journey to success has been about getting out of my comfort zone, that really is what it's been about. Have you heard that saying, "You can't keep doing the same things and expect different results?" Yeah, well that was me. And I was over it. Anyone that knows me, knows that I'm an introvert at heart. I'm one of those people who, just a few years ago, feared public speaking more than death itself. I seriously used to get panic attacks anytime I had to speak in front of anyone, be it five people or a hundred. I was not one to go by myself to an event where I didn't know anyone. I almost didn't go to this conference because it meant I was going to have to go by myself—in a sea of five hundred women. But that little voice in my spirit was practically yelling at me to go . . . so I did.

There are so many opportunities that have manifested for me simply by doing that one uncomfortable thing, attending a conference by myself. Not only did I meet amazing people who are now my friends, but I connected with a dynamic coach who helped me push through many of my fears and start my own business which aligns with my purpose and passion—empowering mothers to build stronger foundations for their families.

I founded Moms 'N Charge in 2012 because it was initially a need that I had for myself. There was a point in my life when I wasn't in charge of anything, and I needed to take back control of me. While I wanted to be there for everyone else, I had to learn how to show up for myself first. I knew there were other moms out there who were battling the same issues that I was, and I wanted to help them take charge of their own lives. As a result, I've built a successful blog and created powerful training workshops for moms to teach them how to FLY (First Love Yourself). When I decided to step out and create my own workshops, there were so many doubts going through my mind: What if no one showed up? What if they hated it? What if I just sucked? Well, if there's one thing I'm sure of, it's that God will find a way to send you confirmation to let you know whether or not you're on the right track.

After receiving glowing testimonials from the first workshop, all I could do was say, "Thank you." I finally felt like I was confident in the path that I was taking. People who attended said things like they "left with a toolbox full of ideas to keep me on the track of loving myself" and that I gave them "tools to use on how to be a fabulous, FLY mom and wife, and still make time for yourself without feeling the guilt."

There is nothing like being of service to others and knowing that your gift is the missing piece to their puzzle. Today, I am able to write this book because when I look in the mirror, I see a beautiful, confident Mom 'N Charge who is ready to take on the world. Are you ready to do the same? It's never easy, but it's necessary if you're going to find your purpose. If I hadn't gone through the struggles and the obstacles, I most likely would have missed the opportunities that have gotten me to where I am today: happy, healthy, and wholeheartedly pursuing my passion.

What is holding you back from creating the opportunities that are waiting for you? Let's get down to business. In order to get to your turning point and create the life you desire, you need to first figure out a few things.

FINDING YOUR SHOES

1. What do you want your life to look like one, two or five years from now? Take a moment to get very clear in your mind (and on paper) what being unstuck would look like before continuing. My coach

always talks about the importance of clarity and how you can't be successful in reaching your goals if you're not clear about where you want your goals to take you to begin with.

TWEET THIS! @WhoseShoesBook
Once you figure out what you want, you can then start to figure out how to get it. #whoseshoes

2. When you think about what you've accomplished in your life so far, what has worked for you and what hasn't? Write down one or two areas you want to currently focus on.

Example: Weight loss

What works: Going to Zumba or other fitness class in a group setting

What doesn't work: Trying to workout at home by myself (no accountability/sense of community)

3. What do you need to let go of before you can focus on your goals (Are there activities you need to cut back on? People you need to eliminate from you circle)?

4. What would you do if you were an expert in the area of your prospective field?

5. What would you do if you had all the money, time and, resources you wanted and needed at your finger tips?

6. What would you do if you were fully confident in your skills and talent?

7. What is one thing you've been avoiding but know you should do? Hint: The very thing you're running from is quite possibly what you should be doing.

8. Write down the fears that are keeping you from going after that opportunity you've been dreaming about.

Once you've written down your greatest fears, rip up the piece of paper and throw it away. Why? Because when you focus on your fears, you lose focus on your purpose. FEAR = False Evidence Appearing Real. Fears are meant to keep you stuck. The only way to get unstuck is to work right through them.

9 FINDING AND LIVING YOUR PASSION

JULIAN

There is no passion to be found playing small—in settling for a life that is less than the one you are capable of living. —Nelson Mandela

Did you know that the vast majority of U.S. workers (70%) are unhappy and unsatisfied at work? That's according to the 2013 State of the American Workplace Report, which surveyed more than 150,000 full- and part-time workers in 2012. That's a pretty eye-opening statistic. It made me wonder why that number was so high. To me, it signaled that the vast majority of people are probably not living out their purpose. I know for a fact that you can't be fulfilled unless you are following your heart's calling.

However, this is often difficult to do when you have other people's expectations to live up to. As most parents do, mine had very high expectations for me. As hard workers themselves, they set the standard for us to follow. Add the additional layer of our African culture to the mix and you've got yourself a doozy. Being high achievers and goal-oriented was what was expected of my siblings and me. We all heard the stories of how my parents had to not only pay for their own primary education in Uganda, but unlike here, they didn't have school buses, so they had to walk miles and miles to and from school. Some days the story was three miles, others it was ten. It changed depending on which one of us they were lecturing (I mean, instilling work ethic in) that day.

Given all that, we were expected to become doctors, lawyers, accountants, or engineers. Something that paid a lot of money. I appreciate the fact that there are people who are called to those professions and are very passionate about them; they just weren't for me. For as long as I can remember, I've always loved art and design. Growing up, I practically slept with a pencil and paper in my hand and was always creating something. In high school, I developed a love for graphic design when I discovered I could marry technology to my love for art. I even wrote a paper in my senior year about how I wanted to use design to change the world. I was very clear on what I wanted to do, and my family will tell you that once I put my mind to something, that's it. Good luck talking me out of it.

Did I mention that my parents were African? In our culture (and I'm sure many others can relate), the arts are not a respected career choice. They are frowned upon and looked at as frivolous; they carry the stereotype of the starving artist. When I began applying to colleges, Mom and Dad expected me to attend an Ivy League school. As class valedictorian, I had my choice of schools to attend, including Princeton, but they didn't have my major at the time. So I decided to go to Marymount University, a small liberal arts college that had a strong design program.

You would have thought I had committed armed robbery. Unable to convince me to change my mind (and provide them with Ivy League bragging rights), my parents stopped talking to me for at least a month after I made that decision. I imagine all they were thinking was, "Eh, eh . . . our poor daughter with all those brains is using them to become a painter." What were they going to tell their friends? And what in the world was graphic design anyway?

It wasn't until I graduated and got my first job at a major global organization, making a lot of money doing what I had studied, that my parents officially reclaimed me as their daughter. Okay, maybe I'm exaggerating a little, but I think they held their breath throughout my college years until they could be assured I was able to obtain gainful employment. That was okay though (Mom, Dad, no hard feelings), because in my mind's eye, I already saw my vision—which was something that no one else but God could dictate or understand.

I eventually left the organization to start my own design firm, and by following my passion for design, I have had the opportunity to work on life-changing projects, travel the world, meet incredible people, and be fulfilled doing what I do for a living, while serving my clients.

In 2013 God let me know that it was time to move on to the next chapter of my life. It meant letting go of the old (my design firm that I had worked so hard to establish) and ushering in the new—my Bold & Fearless blog and brand (www.boldandfearless.me). It was time for me to let go of the vision that was for that particular season in my life and be willing to move on to something that would serve an even greater good.

Through Bold & Fearless, I have been able to write about my journey to where I am and how I got here; provide concrete tips on how to find and fulfill your passion and build your brand; and ultimately inspire change through culture, creativity, and communication. When I launched the blog—which was a very scary thing for me because I was no longer hiding behind client work to establish who I was as a professional—my spirit literally sang. And it's been singing ever since. Because I finally embraced the "updated" vision God had put in front of me, and I was already hearing from others about how what I wrote about in my blog was making a positive impact on them.

Just the other day, I was speaking to a male friend of mine who told me that at times when he's on the grind working hard on his business, if there's a moment of doubt or frustration, he'll think about being "Bold & Fearless" and push through whatever he needs to push through to get to the other side. *That's* what it's all about! That's how I know I'm walking in my purpose. But I have to say that for almost three years prior to launching Bold & Fearless, I felt like I was meandering aimlessly through life, my purpose had become extremely fuzzy, and doubts were chasing me down, trying to overtake me.

You see, I hadn't realized it, but I had plateaued in my own company! I had accomplished just about every goal I had set out to reach, worked on just about every type of project I had ever wanted to work on, and was in denial about my lack of enthusiasm for the work I was now doing. The thrill, the challenge, the *passion* was gone. But wait, how could I be bored when I was the one who had started the company and established the vision? How could it be time to shut down something that I had poured blood, sweat, tears, and a whole lotta money into? How could I just walk away from something I knew God had His hand in every step of the way? Even my business partner pointed out to me that maybe it was time to move on, shut it down, do something new. I wasn't hearing it.

Remember how Christine talked about "holy discontent" in Chapter Two? The reason it took me so long to recognize it for what it was, was because I didn't think it would happen to me in a venture I started. I'm here to tell you, it doesn't matter whether or not it's your "baby." God can ask you to move from a certain situation when He wants to move you to the next level. In my case, He allowed me to stew in my own "stuff" until I was forced to be still enough to really hear what He was trying to tell me.

One day, I decided to just surrender. I was tired of being frustrated from not landing the kind of work I used to, working on projects that I dreaded but did anyway just to pay the bills, and doubting whether I was really capable of fulfilling the purpose that I *thought* God meant for me. This was a very difficult place for me to be: unsure, confused, and full of doubt. Especially since, pretty much all my life, I had always been sure of what my plan and purpose were. For the first time, I had no clue. Or so I thought.

But here's the great thing about being a divine spirit in a physical body: your spirit knows exactly what you're supposed to do and will act like a compass to get you back on course, even when your earthly mind is choosing to be disobedient. As I settled into the knowledge that God had already mapped out my course and given me every tool to be successful on the journey, I found peace.

And what I did next was absolutely key to becoming excited about life again. I invested in a beautiful bright red journal and began to write. I wrote down what made me happy. I thought about the occasions and projects in my life that had brought me the most fulfillment and joy and wrote those down. I dusted off old plans—things I had in the back of my mind for *years*—and gave them a second look. Then I wrote out what I knew to be my mission statement for my life based upon everything else I had written. Looking at the twenty or so pages I filled up over the course of a weekend, I thanked God; for the first time in several years, I was on fire again. And have been ever since.

As I completed this exercise in clarity, it dawned on my that my mission and my passion for empowering and inspiring others through culture, creativity, and communication had never really changed. What had changed was the platform I was to use for fulfilling my mission. Talk about an aha moment. Duh! Why hadn't I recognized that before? Why had it taken me so long to realize what was right in front of me?

Well because, admittedly, I can be a little hard-headed at times. Let me tell you, tunnel-vision is not a good thing. It's usually how you miss out on the doors God is trying to open for you, because you're so busy trying to climb through windows you have no business in, in a house that you've outgrown. Once I realized God was doing a new, more exciting thing in my life, I was ready to let go of my old shoes and get fitted for my new ones. This included making the major decision to close down my design firm and giving my full attention to this new chapter in my life. I haven't regretted one moment of it.

If you were to ask yourself what you're really passionate about and would do even if you didn't get paid for it, would the answer reflect how you're living your life now and the work you're doing? If the answer is yes, congratulations! You can skip the rest of this chapter. If the answer is no, then stick with me so we can work that out.

Examine: 1) What it is that you're really passionate about, and 2) Why you're not doing it. Our emotions are great clues to our hearts' desires. Desires that God programmed into our DNA. I've learned that:

TWEET THIS! *@WhoseShoesBook*
God never gives us a vision He won't help us bring to life. #whoseshoes

In fact, while I was doing my morning meditation one day, He gave me this message:

TWEET THIS! *@WhoseShoesBook*
"You are responsible for bringing your heavenly purpose into earthly reality." #whoseshoes

How many times do we doubt what we are called to do because we fear our own inadequacies in completing the task? Change your perspective and recognize that if you were called to do it, God already has the tools and resources prepared for your use. He's just waiting on you to walk in that knowledge.

As you transform your life, you will have to very consciously transform your thinking. If you're not doing what you're passionate about, then whose dream are you really living? Is it your parents' or other relatives'? Your spouse's? Your friends'? What matters most to you? What is that thing, that dream, that goal that keeps you up at night and gets your blood pumping with the possibilities?

By the time you finish this book, my hope for you is that you will give yourself permission to walk boldly into the life that the world is waiting for you to live—regardless of your fears. I now understand that being fearless doesn't mean that you have no fear. I actually think that fear is necessary to push you past your comfort zone into your audacity zone. Rather:

TWEET THIS! @WhoseShoesBook
Living fearlessly means fearing less that which you don't know than you do dying without using your gifts to light up the world. #whoseshoes

So let's get ready to light it up!

FINDING YOUR SHOES
Let's start by writing down the answers to these questions:

1. Define your passion.
- What three things are you most passionate about?

- What are you good at?

- When do you feel the most joy and fulfillment?

- If you're not in a career that you enjoy, why is that?

- What is really holding you back from doing what you're passionate about? This is not the time to make excuses or play the blame game.

TWEET THIS! @WhoseShoesBook
If you can't take accountability for where you are, you will never get to where you want to be. #whoseshoes

2. Visualize.

Now that you've written down what your dreams and goals are, it's important to see them happening and unfolding in your mind's eye. Find a quiet place where you can focus on envisioning whatever it is you want to manifest in your life. Imagine how it feels to reach that goal, whether it's starting your own business, running a marathon, or writing your first book. How will it feel when you cross the finish line? Create a vibrant, three-dimensional mental picture, and keep that vision in your mind on a daily basis to push you forward until it becomes a reality.

I encourage you to create a vision board. A vision board is a board that captures a physcial illustration of your dream for your life. On it, you can include everything from places you want to go, to people you want to meet, and things you want to have. Your only limit is your imagination. There is something powerful about seeing what you want your life to look like, having it in front of you where you can see it every day. You can use whatever materials you want for your board. Make it large enough that you can fit everything on there that's important to you. I've used magazine clippings, three-dimensional items from the craft store, found objects, stock photos—whatever speaks to me.

When you're done, put your vision board somewhere you can see it every day, where it will motivate you. The most important thing is to believe that you can be and achieve every single thing you put your mind and your heart into. Become so full of faith that you crowd out doubt.

TWEET THIS! @WhoseShoesBook
You've got to have mustard seed faith. (Luke 17:6) #whoseshoes

3. Take the first step towards your vision.

As you think about what you're passionate about and how you really want to spend your time, remember that this is a process. What you're doing now may be what's paying the bills, and that's okay. I'm not asking you to quit your day job today. What I am saying is that even while you're working full time, you can still find ways to begin pursuing your dream on the side. It comes down to how badly you want it, and if you're willing to do the work to get there.

I love what Will Smith said in an interview. "I've never really viewed myself as particularly talented. Where I excel is ridiculous, sickening work ethic. While the other guy is sleeping, I'm working. Where the other guy is eating, I'm working." Just because you have a vision, doesn't mean you can wave a magic wand and all of a sudden your dream is now reality. It takes hard work to realize that dream.

Once you've figured out what you're passionate about, *write it down*. The Bible says, "Write the vision and make it plain." There is power in writing things down. When I first started my design firm,

I wrote down everything I wanted to accomplish in the first three years. Being the person that I am, I filed that information away and didn't look at it again until a couple of years later. And then I laughed, because without even looking at my list, I had subconsciously realized just about every goal I had written down.

Dreams are goals with a deadline. Figure out the top three to five things you need to do to live out your passion, put deadlines on them, and start working towards them. Don't try to eat the whole elephant at once. Make sure your goals are reasonable, while still stretching you, so that you don't get discouraged if you don't reach them because you were trying to do too much in an unrealistic time frame. In other words, don't plan on $10 million in revenue in your first three months of being in business. I can't stress enough how important it is to write your goals down. And then *act*. For "Faith without works is dead." (James 2:14-26)

10 YOUR EXTERNAL TRANSFORMATION

CHRISTINE

Wholistic transformation radiates from the inside, out. Take time to love all of you because when you look good, you feel good. —Christine St. Vil

So far we've talked a lot about the internal changes you need to make and evaluate within, your internal transformation. But for some people, myself included, your journey starts with your external transformation. How do you feel about yourself on the outside? How do you show up for yourself? How do you not show up for yourself when you're not looking and feeling your best?

Come on, y'all know what I'm talking about. When your clothes don't fit like they used to or you can't get an appointment with your hairdresser to get that mane under control, it changes the trajectory of any plans you have. You might have planned to go to a party or gathering with some friends, and if you haven't been out in a while, then you want to go all out, do it up, and turn up. The only problem is you're feeling like a hot mess! Trust me, I've been there, done that, and ain't even trying to go back!

Before I became a stay-at-home mom, and was still working in corporate America, I was fly and very confident of that fact (not in a cocky way, but just in a finally-feeling good-about-myself kind of way). Even when I was pregnant with my first two children, I still rocked it out. I took pride in what I was wearing and in my overall appearance. I never walked out of the house like I just rolled out of bed (unless I was just grabbing the mail). While I had to wear suits to work almost daily, I didn't mind because I enjoy dressing up and I loved the way I felt when I did.

We all know that as women, when we look good (and we know it), we usually feel good. If our hair's not done, then we're not going to put on our cute clothes. If our hair *is* done, then we're going shopping for that cute dress we saw last week. We love to feel beautiful. And yes, as a mother of three and wife of eight years, I still want to look fly. Even now, I get butterflies in my stomach when my husband compliments me on something I'm wearing or just on how I look in general. And my eyes nearly tear up when my daughters (especially my middle one) tell me, "You're so beautiful mommy." When was the last time someone complimented you on your external appearance, and it just made you feel all high-school-girly again?

When I became a stay-at-home-mom, things gradually started to change in that department. For the first time in a really long time, my external appearance started to reflect my inner turmoil. I used to be able to hide my insecurities with my smile and my style, but that was no longer the case. So many doubts took over my mental space and left me feeling like I had made the wrong decision about leaving my job. I began to feel like a failure for bailing out. How in the world was I going to handle being a full-time stay-at-home-mom?

I didn't really feel like I could share this with anyone, so I kept a lot of it to myself. And just as it was eating me up inside, it began to show on the outside. I stopped paying attention to what and how I was eating. Instead of losing weight after I had my third child, I began to gain even more weight. By this point, I was wearing a size twelve nearly a year after I had my daughter. (My average size, even into motherhood, had been an eight.) I was nearly forty pounds overweight and I couldn't even hide behind the fact that I had "just had a baby" anymore. I had to take responsibility for my own actions and my own health. You know how you reach for that last cookie, knowing good and well you have no business doing so? Yeah, I still struggle with that.

Slowly, but surely, I had gradually lost my identity to motherhood. I no longer took the time to care about what I looked like, what I was wearing, or what my hair was doing from day to day. Often, I threw on a pair of my husband's shorts and one of his T-shirts when I dropped my son off at preschool. Looking back now, it was seriously a hot mess. But as I explained earlier, when I reached my turning point and saw someone I didn't recognize staring back at me in the mirror, I knew it was time for a change.

I had to come to grips with the fact that while I'm not old, I am older, and with age comes change. For example, I had to recognize that I no longer had the fat-burning metabolism I'd been known for all of my life. I could no longer eat what I wanted when I wanted without it having an immediate affect on my outward appearance. And I was sick and tired of not doing anything about it.

I realized I had to nip this thing in the bud, and the first thing I did was get back to the basics. I got back to doing the things that made me feel good. I declared the year of 2012 to be my year of change, because clearly, I had gotten way too comfortable looking funky and frumpy in my everyday life.

This meant getting back to the person I was before I became a mother. It started with the face that stared back at me in the mirror. Thanks to YouTube, I learned how to correctly apply my eyeshadow, and then I spent an extra five to seven minutes a day putting on make-up before I left the house, simply because it made me feel good. It didn't matter if I was just going to the grocery store or to drop my son at school; it was a habit I had to redevelop in order to give my self-love muscles a workout. Now it's become second nature. Granted,

I don't always have to look like I'm stepping out of *Essence* (well, most of the time I do, just not *all* the time), but I do take a lot more pride now in how I step out in the world.

Speaking of stepping out, starting my natural hair journey was the one thing that really forced me to step out of my comfort zone. Let me just tell you, India.Arie clearly did not mean that song for me when she wrote "I am not my hair," because I nearly had a heart attack when I chopped off all of mine. It initially wasn't by choice, but instead was something I was forced to do when, after one wash (and seven months of transitioning), my hair was a matted, tangled mess. The only option was to cut it off and start from scratch.

I will never forget sitting on my bathroom floor, after I'd finished cutting off my hair and just crying. (Don't judge me.) For some people, like Ms. Arie, it was just hair. But for me, it was my identity. It was who I was. It was what made me, me. Chopping it all off made me realize just how many insecurities I had in just that one small area of my life.

Growing up, I was constantly told I that had a big forehead so I had always covered it up. Well, I couldn't cover up a darn thing after my big chop. I could no longer hide behind anything or anyone. I wish I could tell you that I felt liberated and free. But I actually felt insecure and anxious. At the same time, I knew this change was what I needed to break free of my fears and stand boldly in my own power. Chopping my hair off forced me to command presence when I stepped into a room. Chopping my hair off forced me to stop hiding behind my mask and to embrace the person that I am. It forced me to just get over my insecurities so that I could finally get out of my own way and start living out the purpose that I was placed on this earth to live. I began to embrace myself as a person and got back to loving me!

Now I'm not saying you need to go out and chop off your hair today—unless you want to, of course. But for me, it was that one action I took that propelled my transformation over the past couple of years. Sometimes there are small things, like hair, we've learned to hide behind, and we don't even realize they're holding us back from stepping into our own shoes.

Around the same time that I chopped off my hair, my husband decided to go vegan on me—just when I learned how to make his mama's mac 'n cheese. He started paying closer attention to the foods he ate and started to consume healthier foods. So naturally, I did the same. We started juicing together and finding ways to make good food that was good for us.

During that process, I decided to own up to the fact that I was no longer twenty-one and that my extra "baby weight" was not going to just disappear on its own. And it especially wasn't going to go anywhere if I kept binging on sweets. Sweets have always been my go-to comfort food. I can eat cake if I'm happy, sad, or mad, and it still tastes just as good to me.

But at some point, I got tired of having to squeeze into everything I owned, or worse, not being able to fit clothes that I used to slide on with ease. Can you relate to that? So I made the decision to get serious about my weight loss and to face my poor eating habits. I also had to realize that we were setting the example for our children. I couldn't expect them to take care of their external appearance if it wasn't something that I had been demonstrating myself. I try hard not to be the "do as I say, not as I do" mom. It's so unfair, and it sends mixed signals.

Wouldn't you know that by simply changing my eating habits, I shed nearly thirty pounds and went from a size twelve to a size six in the course of a year. You know I was feeling myself, right? My body was starting to catch up to how I felt about myself on the inside and how I presented myself on the outside. My self-confidence kicked in, and I truly felt like a fly mom and wife, ready to conquer the world.

I'm teaching my kids, especially my daughters, the importance of self-love starting from within so that it is reflected in their external presence. When I see them interacting with each other, and telling each other how beautiful they are, I know that the seeds we are planting are reaping a harvest.

When you watch most makeover shows, they almost always focus on the person within, and the issues that led to whatever the external problem has become. Once they figure that out, they can then get to work on getting things right on the outside to reflect the work that's going on sinside. Often, your external transformation is just as important as your internal transformation. Are you ready to take it to another level?

FINDING YOUR SHOES

Be you. Do you. Love you.

1. Be You.

So often we are focused on what others think we should be, do or feel. Society has managed to dictate what beauty and love should look like. But in actuality:

TWEET THIS! @WhoseShoesBook
Beauty is in the eye of the beholder, and not in the set of our television. #whoseshoes

- What are one or two things you put on that instantly make you feel good?

- When was the last time you purged your closet of items that no longer serve you?

- What items in your closet are keeping you stuck in the past ?

- Take inventory of what is in your closet and release anything that no longer represents who you are.

2. Do you.

Being healthy plays a huge role in our external transformation. How we really feel about ourselves when no one is watching can make or break our transformation. I had to look long and hard at myself in the mirror and take ownership for my weight gain and lack of overall health.

- Are you really happy with your overall health?

- What are some of your fitness goals that you've been putting off until you "have more time?"

- Are you paying close attention to what you are putting into your body? My personal struggle was with sweets. I craved them them all day, every day. But my body didn't agree. Once I made a conscious decision to take better care of my temple, I was able to lose over thirty pounds with ease.

- What are you willing to give up in order to get to where you really want to be in your health and fitness journey?

3. Love you.

It all comes back to how you First Love Yourself. Your external transformation is dependent upon your own self-care and self-love. It starts with you. No one can do it for you. How can you begin to pour love into yourself every day so you can experience wholistic transformation?

11 WHAT'S CULTURE GOT TO DO WITH IT?

JULIAN

It's not who you are that holds you back, it's who you think you're not.
—Denis Waitley

"Why is your hair so short?"

"Why are you talking funny?"

"What is that you're eating? It looks weird."

"Do you have cars in Africa?"

"Did you know Tarzan?"

"What are you *wearing*?"

Believe it or not, these are all questions I heard growing up, and sometimes still hear even now. This chapter is especially personal for me because of how growing up African in America shaped the image I had of myself. It's taken me a while to get comfortable in these shoes, but after doing the work, what I found out was that unless and until you embrace the fundamental core of who you are and the culture you were born into, you will never be truly whole and complete—or comfortable in your own shoes.

Although I am writing from an African perspective, I've come to understand that regardless of what culture you come from—Asian, Hispanic, Caribbean, Latin American—as long as you've encountered the European standard of beauty, you've probably suffered from the need to adapt, assimilate, and try to morph into a standard that is at war with your God-given DNA.

TWEET THIS! @WhoseShoesBook
Until you accept and embrace all of who you are and the culture you were born into, you will never be truly whole and complete. #whoseshoes

For years, I suffered from a warped self-image, low self-esteem, and even embarrassment about who I was and what I looked like because it was so different from everyone else. Or rather, everyone else that I saw in most magazines and on TV. Why is it so difficult for us to accept ourselves as we are, for who and what we are? It's taken me years to come up with the answer, but I was only able to do that after allowing myself to go deep into my past, my subconscious, and my heart.

One of my first recollections of how different I was from my American classmates—Black or White—is from kindergarten. It was picture day at my new school, and I walked into school proudly wearing my African-print dress. It was one of my favorites, and I just knew I was cute. But on top of that, I had my little one-inch afro. In Uganda, as in many African countries, it's the norm for girls to wear their hair extremely short so that they are more focused on their studies than they are on their style. On more than one occasion, I was asked if I was a boy or a girl and given strange looks as I walked around the school in my African garb. It didn't help that I had what was considered in the U.S. to be a boy's name: Julian.

I will never forget one time in third grade, when I decided to take matters in my own hands. Tired of having a "boy's" name and being mistaken for the opposite sex on occasion, I made a subtle change to how I wrote my name on classroom assignments. I went from being "Julian" to being "Juliet." At nine, I thought I had found a brilliant solution to my dilemma. After all, I had only changed two letters in the spelling. I happily wrote "Juliet" on my schoolwork for the rest of that week. My teacher even said to me, "Wow, I see you've changed your name. Juliet is a pretty name." I just nodded my head and smiled . . . until I took all those school assignments home for my parents to review.

Let me take a minute to explain something about African parents. There is no such thing as a "gray area" or an opinion when you are a child, and sometimes even when you're an adult. It is either black or white, right (them) or wrong (you). So when I proudly handed my schoolwork to my Maama (the way we spell it in my language, Luganda), I had no idea what was to come. Still smiling innocently, I waited for her to commend me on my good grades. Instead, her face showed no emotion as she looked at the papers and then back at me. In her accented English, she asked, "Julian, what is this?"

When I heard her tone, my proud smile disappeared.

"Ummm . . . that's my work from school." This wasn't going the way I had envisioned.

Putting the papers in my face and pointing to where I had written my new name, she asked again, "No, I mean what is this?"

Uh oh. "Oh, I just decided to change my name to Juliet." At nine, I hadn't yet mastered the art of knowing when I was being asked a hypothetical question.

Thunderclouds marring her beautiful face she asked, "You decided to do what?!"

"Uh . . . ummmmm . . ." Maybe I better just stay quiet.

My mother didn't even let me finish my stuttering. In that tone your parents use when they want to slap the foolishness out of you, but instead use every ounce of restraint to avoid doing permanent damage, she gritted her teeth and said, "Sit down, get every piece of paper you have with this name on it, erase it, and write in your proper name. I don't know what you were thinking, but don't ever let me see this again. That is the name you were given, and that is the only name I expect to see on your schoolwork from now on."

You didn't argue with Maama. I was just glad I had escaped that episode with my behind still in tact. (You know what I'm talking about.)

Still, all I could think was, "My African parents just don't understand." That was one of many situations throughout my life where I fought to straddle two cultures, two continents: the one I was born in, and the one I was living in. Figuring out who I was and where I fit in between those worlds, while being accepted in both, was a juggling act. I became a chameleon. When I was with my American friends, I tried to act and look as American as possible. When I got home, it was a different world. I toned down my "Americanism," brought on the accent, and practiced my African culture—which I was still ashamed of outside my home. A very similar experience to my sister's.

It wasn't until I became a teenager and had the opportunity to travel the country performing at venues like the Kennedy Center, as part of an all women's East African performing arts company, that I began to really appreciate and understand the value of my cultural heritage. Joyfully expressing the music and dance of East Africa improved my self-esteem, gave me greater empathy for and perspective on other cultures. It instilled in me the confidence to embrace life with a clear understanding of who I am and what I am capable of.

Now that I'm older and have my own child, I understand even more so the importance of passing on your cultural legacy—the language, the customs, the history. And I see the impact that it has had on my daughter. At ten, she is self assured, well-liked, articulate (sometimes a little too much), and secure in who she is. I strongly believe that her knowing, appreciating, and celebrating her roots, has given her the foundation to be proud of who she, is no matter where she is.

If you are of a different culture or ethnicity than the majority of those around you, I can't stress enough how important it is to your emotional, psychological, and even spiritual well-being to learn to embrace your roots. As I performed around the country, teaching people about East Africa, I found something remarkable happened. The pride and self-assurance that I displayed on stage caused others to think highly of my heritage. It was no longer strange; it was interesting and exciting. They wanted to learn more. Cool.

I now use culture as a platform, not only to celebrate and embrace who I am, but as a point of common ground that allows me to connect deeply with others who have experienced the same shame I used to feel before I understood just how amazing, beautiful, talented, and special I am in all my Africanness. After all,

TWEET THIS! @WhoseShoesBook
If God had wanted us to all look alike, He would have created us all the exact same way. #BeYou #whoseshoes

I recently came across a story that circulated on the Internet about a Chinese woman who was sued by her husband for giving birth to an ugly daughter. I shook my head in disgust when I found out that he won the lawsuit. But was even more saddened when I read that he won because the wife admitted to having $100,000 worth of plastic surgery to provide her with her artificial features, translating into what she had been indoctrinated to believe was beautiful. Although this was an extreme case, at some point you've got to be willing to remove the weave, the lashes, the makeup, and the heels and allow all of you to come to the table. If you don't, you'll always live in fear of being found out and accused of being a fake.

For many of my sisters from parts of Africa, the Caribbean, and the rest of the Diaspora, the practice of skin bleaching has become the norm in an effort to meet expectations that are literally making us sick. The chemicals in these skin-bleaching concoctions have been proven to cause all kinds of health problems, including cancer. A quick trip to Google will yield thousands of results. Not to mention the fact that the hair industry is making billions off of our insecurities about allowing our natural hair to shine through. If my sister Christine could do it and go *au naturale*, as much of a diva as she is, then so can you. I don't think there's anything wrong with wanting to switch up your hairstyle every once in a while and give it a break, but if you feel that your ability to be accepted in society revolves around how long and straight your tresses are and how far you can fling that mane, there are probably deeper issues there. This issue was magnified when I went to Senegal several years ago as part of a delegation for an international festival of arts and culture.

I was excited about my first visit to West Africa in 2010; however, as myself and my colleagues and I traveled around Dakar, Senegal over the course of a week, we began to notice something very strange. And it was prevalent throughout our entire trip—so much so that most of the people in our group, male and female, commented on it. No matter where you went (and we covered a lot of ground on that trip) 99.999999% of the women wore a hair weave. It seemed so odd to me that I decided to count the number of women out of the hundreds, if not thousands, I encountered on that trip, that *weren't* wearing a weave. Six. That was it. Six.

Because Senegalese women had always been known for their intricate hair braiding and styling, and even have a style of braids named after them, it came as a shock to now see the vast majority of them covering up what I knew to be their crowning glory. I definitely wasn't the only one who thought it was extreme. One of my male colleagues facetiously commented, "Somewhere in Senegal, there's a herd of wild horses running bald." It was that serious.

Now before you start getting up in arms about my observations, I want to reiterate what I said earlier. I don't think there's anything wrong with wanting to switch up your hairstyle every once in a while to give it a break, but if you feel your ability to be accepted in society revolves around how long and straight your tresses are, there are probably deeper issues there.

I could go on about the damage we do to ourselves in trying to meet impossible standards of beauty that were imposed on us by a culture that was not our own, but that's another book. The bottom line is, the challenge of cultural assimilation and acceptance of our own differences is a universal theme. The crazy thing is, often the people who you want to imitate, actually want to emulate you!

I don't know any woman who, in the process of figuring out who she really was, hasn't wanted to change something about herself physically. Lord knows I've been there—wanting smaller lips, narrower hips, and lighter skin than I was in; never mind wanting to change my last name from Kiganda to Brown (wasn't trying that again). Learning to become comfortable in our own shoes goes beyond just our external features, though.

It means not being ashamed when you bring your lunch to work and your colleagues don't recognize the traditional food you're eating. Use it as an opportunity to educate. It means not feeling like you have to over-maintain and try to keep your hair right and tight, your nails always brand new, and your lashes always on. For me, it meant being able to proudly proclaim, "Uganda!" when people asked me where I was from, as opposed to saying DC to avoid embarrassing questions like, "Do you live in trees in Africa?" It means using every encounter with cultural ignorance as an opportunity to bridge the cultural divide, while empowering and encouraging others to embrace their own heritage. As Eleanor Roosevelt so wisely stated, "No one can make you feel inferior without your consent."

Over the years, as I embarked on this path of total self-acceptance, I came to appreciate even more the fact that—despite our (mostly silent) protests—my parents made it a point to make sure my siblings and I knew our language, our heritage, and our culture. (Thanks Mom and Dad.) I now recognize what a gift it is to be able to trace my ancestry back centuries if I were to make the effort, because I know exactly where I'm from. I am grateful for an almost automatic bond that happens with other brothers and sisters from similar backgrounds because we understand each other without saying a word. The road to get to where I am today—completely secure in who I am and proud of my Ugandan and Rwandese heritage—was not an easy one. Even now, I still encounter ongoing ignorance about Africa that I write about on my blog ("You're from Africa?! I Bet You had a Pet Zebra . . .), but instead of getting upset and frustrated about those things I can't control, I use them as teachable moments on this journey we call life.

Fortunately, along this journey, I've met wonderful angels and had life-changing conversations with God that affirmed how amazing I was just as I was. And only by embracing and learning to love all of me—chocolate skin, full lips, wide hips, coiled hair, and African flair—would I ever be able to confidently and proudly walk purposefully into my destiny.

FINDING YOUR SHOES

1. Assess.

Where in your past did you learn to be ashamed of your cultural heritage or appearance? How has it affected you as an adult? With this one, you'll have to dig deep, because often, we're not even aware of some of the things we do to camouflage the parts of ourselves we are ashamed of, but don't want to admit.

Write in your journal about incidents or circumstances that have played a part in your understanding of who you are as it pertains to your heritage. Accept them for what they are: your past. Take the time to pray for God to help you heal from them so that you can move on to creating a different future for yourself. This is the most important step in this process. Without it, the others will be extremely difficult. Remember, you can't heal what you won't reveal.

2. Affirm.

If you have never taken the time to look in the mirror and tell yourself that you are amazing just as you are, this may be a hard one for you. It's unfortunate when we don't recognize the Divine that lives within each of us, regardless of where we're from or what we look like. It's taken me a long time to accept all of me, and I'm so glad I did. Because I've accepted me, I walk in that confidence that I'm exactly who God created me to be—no more, no less—in spite of what other people may think.

Here's your prescription: take time every day to look at yourself in the mirror and tell yourself how beautiful, amazing, fearless, capable, and whatever other adjectives you can come up with to describe yourself, you are. My sister and I both stress this because it works, and it's a critical part of finding the shoes God made for you. By accepting and loving the core of who you are, you will have more confidence in celebrating that externally.

3. Research.

Often, we are ashamed of our heritage because we don't understand just how powerful it is. For me, learning about my country and culture through music and dance was life-changing. It helped drastically change my view of who I was and countered all of the negativity that I was fed from different media sources, which mostly gave very one-sided views of Africa.

Take the time to research the country, culture, heritage, region, and powerful individuals who are all a part of the fabric that makes you uniquely you. Go beyond what you've been taught, and seek out your own information. Learn about the trailblazers, the artists, the businessmen and women, the kings and queens, the changemakers—past and present—who have made history and left their mark for you and future generations to use as an example of what is possible when you know who and *whose* you are.

This is one instance where ignorance is not bliss. Unless you know and understand the greatness you come from, you'll find it hard to believe that you are capable of greatness yourself. As you're completing this part of the exercise, which should be ongoing, note that your heritage goes beyond just your immediate family and relatives and is linked to generations upon generations of individuals that came before you. Commit to learning one new thing every week, and make sure to share this important knowledge with your child(ren).

4. Celebrate and educate.

As Maya Angelou said, "I wouldn't take nothing for my journey now." All of these experiences have made me who I am. And because I now understand and embrace that, I can celebrate it without being ashamed. This is the fun part.

Wear clothing that portrays your cultural heritage. Bring food to work or school that you'll be asked questions about, and be ready to answer them. Start using your traditional name and teach people how to pronounce it properly. Introduce Multicultural Day at your school or workplace to, not only teach others about your culture, but to learn about theirs. If you hear an ignorant remark from someone about where you're from, use it as an opportunity to enlighten and educate. I can't tell you how many times I've had to let people know that there was more to Uganda than Idi Amin! I've had many teachable moments like that, but rather than becoming offended, I used it as an opening for dialogue. Most people just don't know more than what's been taught to the them and are often surprised when I share information with them that they otherwise wouldn't have been aware of—like the fact that Uganda was nicknamed the Pearl of Africa because of its natural beauty and lush greenery.

Every interaction with another human being is an opportunity to connect and educate, especially when you visibly and proudly display your heritage.

12 DO IT AFRAID
CHRISTINE

FEAR has two meanings: Forget Everything And Run or Face Everything And Rise. The choice is yours.

While my transformational journey is ongoing, it has been all about working through my fears in a way I never had before. Over the past few years, I've learned the things that scare me the most, are ultimately the things that open doors to my success.

When I left my corporate job, the only exit strategy I had was to take a leap of faith. I knew that my decision to leave was not about me. I knew that I had a purpose and that God was going to use me in a way that wasn't going to make sense to me at the time. Have you ever done something you never imagined yourself doing before? Or, on the flip side, have you held back from doing something you wanted to do simply because fear kept rearing its ugly head?

The year I left my job was a year of reflection and discovery. It was a year of finding my voice and figuring out who I was and what I wanted deep down. It's funny how God prepares you for things and gives you certain skills long before you even know you need them. I realized that my ability to coach and counsel others—which is what I do now with Moms N' Charge—started when I was working in Human Resources.

During this period of discovery, reflection, and growth, I was reading and researching different topics online; one that kept popping up was the phrase "Do it Afraid." "But what the heck does that mean," I would ask myself? How can you do something you're not just apprehensive about, but actually terrified of? Well, it may sound crazy to you, but it's easier than you think. Before we go into the how, I need you to understand this:

TWEET THIS! @WhoseShoesBook
If you're not uncomfortable, you're not growing.
#whoseshoes

And you can't get through transformation while trying to skip over the growth process. Trust me. I tried, and it doesn't work.

People like to say God works in mysterious ways, but I like to say that God works in intentional ways. It may not make sense to us initially, but there is always a master plan behind it.

Take for example, Exhibit A:

Earlier, I mentioned the Get RADICAL Women's Conference. And no, I'm not getting paid to promote this conference, but it's been instrumental in my own transformation. I met the founder, Doreen Rainey, at an event, a few weeks before her 2012 conference. At this point, I had no idea where God was leading me or what I wanted to be when I grew up. When I saw the program and the keynote speakers (Suze Orman, Lisa Nichols, Jillian Michaels), I knew I had to be there. I knew that this was the radical step that I needed to get me closer to achieving my goals and dreams, whatever they were.

In order to get the most out of the conference, I knew I was going to have to register for the VIP experience. When you're unemployed, $700 is a major investment. Shoot! It's a huge investment even when you *are* employed. But I kept hearing that voice confirming that I was moving in the right direction.

Okay, so remember how I talked about being uncomfortable? Well, uncomfortable for me at that time was attending a conference with five hundred strangers. But that's exactly what I did, and I ended up making new friends in the process. (Patting myself on the back right here.)

During the course of the conference, there were several opportunities for attendees to make their way to the microphone in the middle of the room to ask a question or to just share a comment. As deathly afraid as I was of public speaking, I challenged myself that weekend to make my way to the mic, even if it was just to say "hi." It took me a couple of days to get there, but at the end of the conference, I finally got up and shared how grateful I was that I attended and how amazing it was. And guess what? I'm still alive!

Not only that, but as one of my goals for the following year, I wrote that I wanted to be a panelist at the next conference because I was so inspired. And one year later, I was selected as part of the success panel for the RADICAL Success Institute (a business coaching program for entrepreneurs). I almost let fear keep me from submitting my application to speak.

So what is your biggest fear? What is the one thing you would do right now if you knew that success was just on the other side, waiting for you? Let me be real with you. You may never get over your fears. But the more you confront and push through them, the more you will learn how to manage them. As with all things, it just takes some practice.

Moving on to Exhibit B:

After that first conference, I decided to invest heavily in myself, both personally and professionally. I knew that most of what I would be doing business-wise would be heavily dependent upon my faith: not just my spirituality, but my belief in myself. Self-belief is the absolute number one trait needed in order to achieve any level of success as defined by you. It's not enough just to say it. You really do have to believe that you are capable of achieving that very thing that keeps you up at night.

When I initially launched my website (www.momsncharge.com), I wasn't quite sure what I wanted to do. But for whatever reason, I knew that God had paved the way and placed on my heart, that I would carry His message of self-love and empowerment through speaking—the very thing I had been deathly afraid to do all of my life. Boy, I tell ya, He's got the greatest sense of humor! The more I tried to run away from public speaking, the more He slapped me in the face with it. So much so that when I initially launched my website, I launched it as "Speak On Faith." I knew that it was going to take a whole lot of faith in order to stand up and willingly offer to speak in front of crowds. Who does that?!

In the process of undergoing my own transformation, I realized that one of the things I needed to let go of was my fear of public speaking. I knew that God was calling me for a purpose higher than myself, and the only way I was going to get there was if I put all of my trust and faith in Him. It meant that I had to get really comfortable being uncomfortable. That doesn't even sound right, does it? Yeah, I didn't think so either. But this one thought process changed the trajectory of my life and my business. When you learn to "do it afraid," you learn to let go and let God. The more you do that, the more growth you will experience.

In addition to speaking at the Get RADICAL Women's Conference that same year, I also spoke at several other events, taught workshops, conducted live teleconferences and, wait for it . . . became a finalist in a business pitch competition where I had to present in front of four hundred people, including representatives from *Black Enterprise* and Wells Fargo! That was a heck of an experience I will never forget. I may not have won that time, but I gained something even more valuable than the prizes that were awarded to the winner—a shot of confidence that would propel me to the next level of my journey.

And then we have Exhibit C:

The year 2013 was all about me making the decision to get out of my own way. It was about learning how to, not only get out of my comfort zone, but stay away from it as much as possible. Part of that relied heavily on taking charge of different aspects of my own life. I wanted to set the bar so high for myself that by the end of the year I would be able to look back and celebrate all of the ways that I got unstuck. It was about being unapologetic about "who I be."

When I started Moms 'N Charge in 2012, I had anxiety about a lot of things. I doubted myself for so many reasons. Did I have what it takes? Would anyone want to work with me? What would my colleagues think of me? Would people judge me because I didn't complete grad school? What if I failed? What if I was making the wrong decision? The struggle and the doubt is real, y'all. But I remembered a quote that said:

TWEET THIS! @WhoseShoesBook
"Doubt kills more dreams than failure ever will."
#whoseshoes

So with that, I had to keep telling myself that I would never know the answer to any of these questions if I never made the attempt to at least try.

I didn't have much clarity about how I would make money in my new venture. I knew that I would need the support and guidance of a great coach and mentor to help me lay my foundation and get me to where I wanted to be. Over the course of one year, I invested more than $20,000 into personal and professional development for myself (yes, that would be $20,000 American dollars). Talk about scary! I didn't jump at every opportunity thrown at me, rather I was strategic about how and what I invested my money in, always consulting with The Man Above to make sure I was heading in the right direction. I'm not saying you need to go out and invest $20,000 in yourself, but I *am* saying that personal and professional development is an investment that can help you reach your desired level of transformation. Only you can decide what you're worth.

Transformation is all about growth. It doesn't happen overnight. It takes nurturing, patience, and time. For some it might take a little longer than others, but that's okay. It's not a race to see who can get to the finish line first. Instead, think of it as a lifelong marathon. Your goal is to continue to transform your life in every area. Your goal is to continue to learn about yourself, to challenge yourself to grow. Your goal is to find your own perfectly-fitted shoes and walk confidently in them—no permission needed.

FEAR = Fear Everything And Run or Face Everything And Rise. It's your choice. Will you run or will you rise? I chose to rise, and I'll continue to rise every time because I have young children who are looking up to me. I have to set the standard and the example for them. When you are pursuing your purpose, you start to realize that this journey is not about you. It's about using your gift to serve the world in a way that will bring you more fulfillment and peace than fear ever will. So what are you waiting for? Follow the famous words of Nike and "Just do it!" Do it afraid. Do it now.

FINDING YOUR SHOES

Take some time to think about these questions, then pull out your journal and write down your answers:

1. What is the one thing that you are avoiding or running away from?

2. What motivates you?

3. How do you keep yourself stuck?

4. What is one thing that is missing from your life? How could your life be more fulfilling if you had this one thing?

5. What is your dream? Hint: If it doesn't scare you, then it's not big enough.

6. Do you believe in God or the concept of a higher power? How does this impact your life and the decisions you make?

7. What does success mean to you? Keep in mind that it has nothing to do with society or what your family or colleagues think. It's what you believe success means.

8. What do you want the rest of your life to look like?

9. How are you investing time and resources into your personal and professional growth?

10. What do you think are your weakest points?

11. What are your strong points?

Once you've written down your answers, pick the three things that scare you the most. Those are the things you need to start with. Put a deadline on when you want to accomplish those things. For example, the first year I attended the Get RADICAL Women's Conference, I made a goal to be back the following year to speak on the stage, and it happened. The key to "doing it afraid" is to close your eyes and take that leap. The more you step into your fears, the easier it will become to walk boldly and fearlessly in the shoes that God created just for you.

13 CONCLUSION

There is nothing like returning to a place that remains unchanged to find the ways in which you yourself have altered. —Nelson Mandela

Wow! We did it, and you made it through to the end with us! How do you feel? What do you feel? We hope this book helps you along your path of transformation—the one that God ordained especially for you. Our prayer for you is that you will go through the exercises in this book, and continue to nurture, love, and transform yourself into the beautiful butterfly that God created you to be.

TWEET THIS! *@WhoseShoesBook*
You don't need anyone's permission to walk in your power. You just need to trust that, if you leap, faith will catch you. #whoseshoes

We want you to promise that you will show up for yourself and be unapologetic about it. You will say no when you need to; set boundaries for those who have been crossing them; put your needs first on your list of priorities; listen to that still, small voice inside of you; and get rid of that excess baggage. Ask yourself what you want your life to look like one year from now? What commitment and sacrifices are you willing to make in order to get there? We can't promise you it will be be painless, but we can promise you it will be worth it. Are you ready to step into your own shoes?

KEEP IN TOUCH

We want to hear from you! Send us your stories and your pictures as you go through your journey. We will be sharing them and would love to hear about your progress. One thing is for sure: you can do this!

E-mail us at info@whoseshoesbook.com and connect with us on:

@ www.whoseshoesbook.com (Sign up for our mailing list!)

🐦 Twitter @WhoseShoesBook

📷 Instagram @WhoseShoesBook

👍 Facebook   www.facebook.com/WhoseShoesBook

▶️ YouTube at www.youtube.com/WhoseShoesBook

If you're interested in a book signing or having us speak at an upcoming event, contact Mocha Ochoa-Nana at The Oracle Group, mocha@theoraclegroupinc.net.

You can also find us on our personal blogs at:

Christine: www.momsncharge.com; info@momsncharge.com

Julian: www.boldandfearless.me; info@boldandfearless.me

Thank you for taking this journey with us. We look forward to hearing from you!

Be blessed,

Christine & Julian

RESOURCES

Here are some great resources that can help you along your own journey of transformation, many of which were instrumental in ours.

Resources for Rape & Abuse Victims:

National Institute of Justice: *http://www.nij.gov/topics/crime/rape-sexual-violence/Pages/other.aspx*

Rape Abuse Incest National Network: *RAINN.org*

Postpartum Depression

Postpartum Progress: *postpartumprogress.org*

Author Marketing, Promotion & Development

The Oracle Group: *www.theoraclegroupinc.net*

Photography

Eye Imagery Studios: *www.eye-imagery.com (studio photography)*
Kizpics: *www.kizpics.com (event photography)*

Professional Video

Tameka Harris Live: *www.tamekaharrislive.com*

Image Consulting and Styling

The Style Medic: *www.thestylemedic.com*

Makeup Artists

Miranda E. Lee: *www.mirandaelee.com*

Faari Faces: *faari.faces@gmail.com*

Web Design

Craft Web Solutions: *www.craftwebsolutions.com*

African-Inspired Clothing

Nubian Hueman: *www.nubianhueman.com*

Simply Cecily: *www.simplycecily.com*

ABOUT THE AUTHORS

With biology degree in hand, **Christine K. St. Vil** initially considered a career in chiropractic medicine. However, after landing employment in the medical industry, she ultimately chose a fulfilling career in Human Resources. Christine's tremendous drive fueled her rapid promotion as an HR professional in the hospitality industry, and provided her with unparalleled leadership training that has been an asset in her career. As a busy mother of three and rising entrepreneur, this passionate professional is determined to help moms everywhere learn how to F.L.Y. (First Love Yourself) and take charge of their lives through Moms N' Charge (www.momsncharge.com). Driven by her personal experience with postpartum depression, frustration, and guilt after becoming a mother, she is committed to helping other moms avoid that same road. Today, she is living out her dreams through the work she does—teaching mothers everywhere how to create healthier lifestyles for themselves and their families, while still pursuing their own dreams and goals. A sought-after social media expert and speaker with her own rapidly-growing blog, Christine has interviewed celebrities and written popular features for the award-winning websites, BlackAndMarriedWithKids.com and HappyWivesClub.com. She has also partnered with organizations such as the Arthritis Foundation, The National Psoriasis Foundation, and The Better Family to create successful digital media strategies to promote her clients' events and extend their brands. Christine received her BS in Biology from Marymount University.

🐦 & 📷 @MomsNCharge   👍 facebook.com/MomsNCharge

Julian B. Kiganda is a dynamic speaker, writer and, creative consultant who uses her performing arts and brand marketing background to help individuals and organizations around the world realize their vision through her Bold & Fearless brand (www.boldandfearless.me). A native East African, her mission is to inspire youth and adults alike to live out their purpose boldly and fearlessly by embracing culture, creativity, and communication. As a performing artist, and member of a nationally renowned dance troupe, she has showcased the music, song, and dance of East Africa all over the United States and in the Caribbean—with appearances at the Kennedy Center, Smithsonian Museum of African Art, Art Saves Lives Foundation, and numerous other venues. As a multicultural marketing and communications expert, she has created powerful brands which have increased revenues and visibility for businesses and organizations—from the African Union, the Freedom House Museum, and Turner Construction, to the National Park Foundation, the National Urban League, and the African Center for Economic Transformation. She is a co-founder of African Diaspora for Change, an organization which educates and empowers African immigrants and the broader diaspora through culture, dialogue and advocacy (www.ad4change.org). Julian and her work have been featured in various media, including: *The Washington Post,* NBC News, ABC News, AP, Voice of America, *Communication Arts, HOW* Magazine, *Huffington Post*, NPR, *ARISE* Magazine, Black Web 2.0, and many others. She is an active public speaker and mentor and has been invited to speak, present and/or teach at the United Nations, World Bank, the State Department's International Visitor Leadership Program, The Peace Corps, Howard University, Art Institutes of Washington, Alabama State University, and many others. She received her BA in Graphic Design from Marymount University.

🐦 & 📷 @BoldFearless1   👍 facebook.com/BoldandFearless1

Made in the USA
Charleston, SC
06 October 2014